POWerful Memories

POWerful Memories

Augustine Fernandez

Copyright © 2005 by Augustine Fernandez.

Library of Congress Number: 2004097365
ISBN :   Hardcover   1-4134-6888-8
                Softcover   1-4134-6889-6

All rights reserved. No part of this book may be reproduced or transmitted in any form or by any means, electronic or mechanical, including photocopying, recording, or by any information storage and retrieval system, without permission in writing from the copyright owner.

This book was printed in the United States of America.

To order additional copies of this book, contact:
Xlibris Corporation
1-888-795-4274
www.Xlibris.com
Orders@Xlibris.com
25453

Contents

Acknowledgements 9
Preface : A Vanishing Legacy 11

Chapter 1 : Ybor City 13
Chapter 2 : The Army Air Corps 23
Chapter 3 : Cadet Days 27
Chapter 4 : A Dream Denied 30
Chapter 5 : Redirection 32
Chapter 6 : Snake Bit! 36
Chapter 7 : Fire Power! 38
Chapter 8 : Fresh Salmon and Dead Pigs 41
Chapter 9 : Practicing for the Real Thing 45
Chapter 10 : Connecting 47
Chapter 11 : The Real Thing 50
Chapter 12 : A Close Call 59
Chapter 13 : The First to Bomb Berlin! 61
Chapter 14 : Fate Steps In 66
Chapter 15 : Captured! 73
Chapter 16 : Interrogation 78
Chapter 17 : A Kick in the Pants! 82
Chapter 18 : Stalag Luft 1 84
Chapter 19 : Escape Schemes 109
Chapter 20 : Operation Cookhouse Mole 114
Chapter 21 : I Make Myself Useful 119
Chapter 22 : Tunneler 123
Chapter 23 : Cave-in! 127
Chapter 24 : Rocket Launcher 130
Chapter 25 : Barracks Life 133

Chapter 26 : News from a Secret Radio 141
Chapter 27 : Mending a Broken Leg
             the German Way 144
Chapter 28 : Activities 146
Chapter 29 : Morale Booster 149
Chapter 30 : Nazis Tighten Control 151
Chapter 31 : The Red Cross and the YMCA 154
Chapter 32 : Kriegie Humor 156
Chapter 33 : A Long Cold Winter 157
Chapter 34 : The Uninvited! 163
Chapter 35 : The Battle of the Bulge 165
Chapter 36 : Christmas Nostalgia 167
Chapter 37 : An Unexpected Acquaintance
             with Hospital Staff 169
Chapter 38 : Conditions Worsen 178
Chapter 39 : Liberation! 180
Chapter 40 : An Error in Judgment 186
Chapter 41 : Paris! 193
Chapter 42 : Stowaway! 196
Chapter 43 : Going Home 199
Chapter 44 : There's No Place like Home 201

Appendix 205

This book is dedicated to Lori, Joe, John, Marc,
and
Future Generations

Acknowledgements

Without the encouragement of my wife, Esther, this story would never have been written. She prevailed upon me to record the experiences I lived through as a prisoner of war for thirteen months in Stalag Luft 1 near Barth, Germany, during World War II. From my disjointed reminiscing as I looked back after a span of some sixty years, she wove a fairly coherent story.

I would like to acknowledge the help I received from Frau Helga Radau, a current resident of Barth. I contacted her via e-mail and she got me in touch with Ken Wilcox who also was imprisoned at Stalag Luft 1.

While in prison, Ken acquired a camera and had actual photographs of the camp. He generously sent me two discs of prison camp photographs with his permission to use them in my book.

B-17 photographs are courtesy of The 457th Bomb Group Association and The Air Force Heritage Museum.

The book jacket design and pen and ink illustrations were created by Alex Durr Productions, 1305 Virginia Place, Fort Worth, Texas, 76107.

Preface
A VANISHING LEGACY

We, those old dinosaurs of World War II, are fading fast. Before we become entirely extinct, it is my wish to chronicle the true experiences of daily life as a prisoner of war (POW) interned at Stalag Luft 1, a cold, desolate place near the Baltic Sea, with long days and longer nights. Before I tell my tale of dropping from the sky into enemy hands, however, I will provide a brief introduction to my family.

Chapter 1

YBOR CITY

Except for a twist of fate, or the grace of God, I would not be an American citizen. My father was born in Asturias, a province of Spain, during a time of great unrest. Every boy who reached the age of twelve was conscripted into the military for physical training and indoctrination. Before this could happen to my father, José, my grandfather sent him, with the assistance of an underground established for this purpose, to the New World. At the tender age of eleven, and alone, he was put aboard a sailing ship with only one change of clothes, his food for the trip, a bedroll and a few pesetas. The year was 1904, and although the United States and Spain had signed a peace treaty ending the Spanish-American War, hostilities between Spain and Cuba had not yet ceased. When the ship reached Cuba and attempted to enter the harbor at Havana, it was turned away by gunfire. Faced with limited options, the captain and the prevailing winds chose Tampa, Florida.

The Tampa Asturianos took him in, found him a place to stay and a job as a busboy in a local restaurant. He remained there until at the age of thirteen the contemptuous arrogance of a customer pushed him over the edge. He was ladling *caldo Gallego*, a Spanish soup, for the diners when one of them shoved him aside and said, "Get that garbage out of my face!" This unwarranted rudeness so incensed young José that he turned the tureen over and baptized the boor with the rest of the soup. A gentleman from another table observed this incident, came over, gave the boy his card and said, "Come to see me tomorrow." Thus began my father's lifelong work in the Tampa cigar industry.

I think of myself as a fairly macho guy, but I began life as the "baby" of my family, a bonus, I like to believe, born to my parents a little later in their lives. My mother gave me my nickname, Chunchi, and called me her *muñeco de trapo*, (rag doll). She, like my father, was an immigrant from northern Spain. They met in this Land of

Promise, married, and settled down in Ybor City, Tampa, Florida.

My parents were quite ahead of their time. They never resorted to corporal punishment even when, as a six year old, I botched up a visit to my great aunt. While the grown-ups were chatting, I wandered upstairs in the direction of birdsong. I found a homemade aviary on the upstairs porch which contained dozens of canaries singing away. My father had taught me that it was cruel to cage animals so I opened the cages to let the birds fly free—and fly free they did, never to be seen again.

My folks never felt the need to master the English language, and by the time I started school, I hadn't mastered it either. I quickly earned the nickname, *"Qué lo que dijo?"* as that was what I was constantly saying to my classmates. *"Qué lo que dijo? Qué lo que dijo?"* (What did she say? What did she say?) The value of communicating in English became quite clear when I was transferred to another school and the teacher sent me to the office to correct an error on my transfer papers. There the school secretary directed me to sit on a bench with several other boys. Soon the principal, a sturdy lady with fiery red hair, marched us all into her office, administered a thorough spanking to each of us and pointed us back to our classrooms. Dumbfounded by this reception, I slipped in through the back door, and slid down behind my desk as far as I could. A few minutes later I saw the fierce, red-headed lady principal enter. She and my teacher began to scan the room and I sank even farther down, but to my dismay, she spied me. She came back to my desk, and although her words were incomprehensible, I understood from her hugs that this school was not going to be as tough as I had feared. She and I became fast friends.

My Uncle Severino was quite the *caballero*, a star in the local Spanish Little Theater Group. I was given a small part in one of his plays and was eager to acquit myself well. All I had to do was enter and announce, *"Señores y señoras, la cena está servida."* (Ladies and gentlemen, dinner is served.) I practiced before the mirror until I had it down pat. However, when I walked onto that stage and saw what seemed to be thousands of eyes on me, I became like a deer in the headlights, frozen and unable to speak or move. To my humiliation, I actually was removed from the stage by the "hook" ending any acting aspirations I might have harbored.

We kept a succession of cows in the backyard of our modest Ybor City home, and I was very fond of those benign creatures with their large, soulful, brown eyes. I remember a Linda, then a Lucero, and, last, a Nelly. It was my job to milk the cow, and one day when I had a full bucket of milk, I discovered the exciting principle of centrifugal force. I found that I could whirl the bucket around my head and the milk would stay in the pail. I was anxious to share this phenomenon with my dad and I ran toward him shouting, "Papa, watch this!" Unfortunately, at that very moment the handle separated from the bucket and the milk went flying, to the delight of my dog, Beauty, who quickly lapped up this unexpected treat. Papa never said a word. My chagrin was punishment enough! It was also my very tedious job to churn the butter for our table and how I resented it when my brothers slathered butter on their bread at dinner while sending taunting, sidelong glances my way.

Attending school was a privilege in those days. Teachers and especially the principal were highly respected. One day, to my utter astonishment, my teacher drove up to our house and asked to speak to my mother. I knew I was no angel in the neighborhood, pugnaciously taking up for myself when I felt it necessary, and I feared one of my scrapes was about to be reported. I brought a neighbor lady over to serve as interpreter, went across the road, climbed a giant old oak tree which often served as a refuge and perched in the branches until my teacher left and I could learn my fate. Imagine my relief when my mother told me that school personnel wished to double-promote me for my academic performance.

One day, in junior high school, testing limits, I ran down the hall to avoid being late to class. I did not see our principal leaning against the wall until his hand reached out to grab me. My immediate reaction was to duck and accelerate, causing my repeatedly washed shirt to rip and come away in his grip. I didn't slow down until I reached home. I quickly slipped past my mother who was washing clothes on the back porch, donned a clean shirt and ran back to school. When I entered my classroom, I was late and sweating profusely. I made up a tale of being ill and nauseated in the boys' bathroom which my dear sympathetic teacher did not question. The principal scoured the school looking for a shirtless culprit, but that time I got away with one.

In our neighborhood there was a defunct laundry which had gone bankrupt during the depression. The structure was purchased by a gentleman, Mr. Swett, who had come to south Florida from Portland, Maine. He converted the rundown laundry into a soap factory. The old building had a tin roof and was as hot as Hades inside, but I was happy to get a Saturday job there. We made bleach, laundry soap and shampoo. My pay was one dollar, but I could earn more by adding other tasks such as filling and labeling shampoo bottles at the rate of one cent each. Sometimes, and I hate to own up to this, but I wouldn't want anyone to think me a better kid than I was, sometimes, after a long steamy workday, I would strip, chin myself down into a vat of shampoo and shower off before heading home. I admit my behavior was reprehensible, but it sure felt good!

Mr. Swett was a well-educated, kindly man, a devout Christian Scientist, and he took a fatherly interest in my welfare. He never could get my nickname right though, and always called me "Chauncey." My family was Catholic and we attended Catholic services for weddings, baptisms and funerals. Otherwise, in those depression years, there was too much to be done on Sunday for regular churchgoing. Mr. Swett, probably rightly concerned for my lack of religious training, would pick me up and take me with his family to Christian Science meetings where he often served as a lay preacher. His three sons, Clinton Tucksbury, Manson York, and Robert Ellsworth and I became lifelong friends. In addition to the Christian Science meetings, there were weekly revival meetings held in tents in the woods outside of town. The Swett family often attended these, taking me along. Usually those preachers were of the fire and brimstone genre and some members of the congregation got so worked up they would begin to "speak in tongues" and sometimes collapse in the aisles. The townspeople called these fervent souls "Holy Rollers." One day I had a very different experience. Billy Graham was the revival preacher. I was captivated by the power and eloquence of his words. His sermon was a mind opener. After that, whenever Billy Graham was in the pulpit, I was sure to be there.

My brothers, Francisco (Frank), and Fernando (Ferdie), were both generally very good to me, protective and indulgent. The Great Depression of the thirties made it necessary for them to leave school after finishing junior high to become wage earners. They were determined, however, that I should be able to complete high school and saw to it that I had those adolescent necessities such as nice clothes and the use of an automobile from time to time, along with the dollar I earned working in the soap factory each weekend.

Football was my passion in high school. I was a running back on offense and a linebacker on defense. Being something of a football star certainly had its rewards. I found myself popular with the high school girls when I was allowed to begin dating, but I had definite boundaries set by my family, especially my brother, Frank, whose car I used. I remember one night picking up my date for a football banquet that her mother cautioned me, "Now, Augustine, we expect Doris Anna home by eleven, but absolutely no later than twelve."

"Don't worry, ma'am," I replied. "I have to be home by ten thirty!"

I was offered a football scholarship to the University of Florida following my senior year provided that I could gain at least twenty pounds. Life was good. I had a loving family, friends, and football, with favorable prospects for my future. Just before I graduated at midyear, however, my life, along with millions of others, changed completely. With the Japanese attack on Pearl Harbor in Honolulu, Hawaii, December 7, 1941, we found ourselves at war.

War Declaration Certain

Chapter 2

THE ARMY AIR CORPS

My buddies and I were all eager to come to the aid of our country and dispersed, each to enlist in his chosen branch of the military. I saw myself as a Navy pilot and headed to St. Petersburg, Florida, to sign up as a naval cadet. Unfortunately, there I learned that if I did not make it through pilot training, I would spend the rest of the war in a sailor uniform with its bell bottom trousers boasting thirteen buttons. That picture did not match my self-image, so I pulled a one-eighty and joined the Army Air Corps.

I reported to Camp Blanding, just southwest of Jacksonville, Florida, where all of us, the young hopefuls, were subjected to every test ever devised. We were put through physical fitness tests, endurance tests, and stress tests. We were screened for tuberculosis, heart problems, hearing problems and vision problems. Any candidate who was found to be color-blind was promptly rejected. We were quizzed on English language proficiency and knowledge of current events. We were even questioned regarding our sexual orientation and if those answers were deemed inappropriate the rejection notice was again quickly forthcoming.

I passed all the preliminary examinations and my next assignment was the Cadet Training Program at Maxwell Army Air Base, Montgomery, Alabama, where I was checked in to begin basic training and assigned to a dormitory. In the army the alphabet determined who your dormitory bunkmates would be. My letter was "F" and I, Fernandez, found myself with Finn, Finnegan, Flagherty, Flannigan, and Foote, all Irishmen. I remember them as a bunch of great guys.

I was selected to be a cadet officer and was issued a sword as part of my uniform. One evening I was practicing my thrusts and parries and just as I wheeled and thrust, Figa, a cadet from the next room entered. He suffered a slightly pierced buttock. I was demoted and spent the rest of my cadet time as a platoon sergeant.

Training was rigorous—up at 5:00 a.m., five minutes to shower, shave, brush teeth and dress, fall out into formation and march to breakfast. Classes in about every course a college freshman would experience were mandatory, with some extras included. We studied English, history, chemistry and math. In addition we had lectures in map reading, escape and evasion, and my nemesis, Morse code. Some of the guys were naturals in code and could even converse with one another using only dah-dit-dahs. For me, however, it was the single most difficult system I had to master. By sheer memorization I did get through it.

One of our survival courses required us to be prepared to bail out over open water. We were advised to try to gauge when we were about 50 feet above the surface to release the parachute harness and throw our arms up so that we would hit the water vertically, minimizing injury. Once we were in the water, other skills came into play which could only be mastered through experience. Wearing full flight gear including helmets, boots, and life jackets which we called Mae Wests for obvious reasons, we were taken to the base swimming pool where each of us, in turn, had to climb up to the three-meter diving board, have a cable attached, be swung out to the middle of the pool and dropped. Once we bobbed up to the surface, we had to inflate the Mae West, one side at a time, by pulling levers allowing the life jacket to fill automatically. We then had somehow to get ourselves to the side of the pool. When we were fairly proficient in this routine, we were dropped into the pool with a Mae West which malfunctioned, making it necessary to clear an air tube, grab a lungful of air and blow as we were sinking for the second time. If we got enough air into the jacket to bring us back up to the surface we could continue to blow until the life jacket was full. I saw cadets wash out of the entire program because they could not make themselves go through this training. I could not really swim, but I could dogpaddle. That was a skill I learned at about age twelve when my buddies, Bobby and Manson Swett, not believing that a boy who lived in a city on the Gulf Coast couldn't at least tread water, threw me, over my strong protests, into the Hillsborough River. It was, literally, sink or swim!

Chapter 3

CADET DAYS

In the cadet program, hazing was the order of the day. Underclassmen were required to eat a "square meal" in the short time allotted for dinner. The fork must be brought straight up to mouth level and then straight in. Eyes must remain on a point and never stray to the plate, or anywhere else, or the new cadet risked a reprimand, "Mister! Are you planning to buy the real estate?" and in responding lose valuable eating time.

I was a pretty rugged guy, but not at all on the tall side, standing only 5'6" at best. Upperclassmen took delight in accosting me with, "Mister! Are you standing in a hole? Mister! Do you know the top of your head is flat? Mister! Are you listening to me? Everything I say seems to be going right over your head!"

My only response was, "Yes, sir!" or, "No, sir!" No elaboration allowed.

Drinking a coke during the day was absolutely prohibited, but the thought of that ice cold elixir sliding down my throat after a seven hour march with a full pack was irresistible. The bathroom was our only sanctuary—upper classmen were not permitted to enter under any circumstances although they could stand outside and berate us through the door. With great cunning we devised ways to slip a coke into the bath and occasionally were able to enjoy a cold shower inside as well as out.

Liberty was eagerly anticipated and on Saturdays we piled into buses for a night on the town. The two main hotels were always crowded and securing a room was quite a prize, so it was not unusual to find six or eight guys bunking together. In addition to the usual weekend activities such as girl watching and beer sampling, we sometimes found an opportunity to retaliate on those despised upperclassmen. Our favorite trick, which delighted our sophomoric hearts, required us first to scan the hotel opposite ours with binoculars to see if anyone over there was scanning us. If the coast was clear, we filled a "pro" with water, surreptitiously unlatched the screen, took careful aim and bombed the unsuspecting pigeon below.

Chapter 4

A DREAM DENIED

I cleared the hurdles of pre-flight training and academics and at long last found myself in the pilot's seat of a Stearman PT-17. It was a dream come true but sadly, not one destined to last. My short stature interfered with the necessary unobstructed view of all sides. Since sitting on a pillow would be frowned upon, I tolerated the inconvenience until one day coming in for a perfect three-point landing I felt a slight jolt—just a slight jolt, mind you—before touching down. To my dismay I found that I had grazed the top of a Coke truck whose driver was inexplicably taking a shortcut across the runway. The "Brass" did not take an optimistic view of the occurrence, and after, as they assured me, much consideration on their part diverted my career to other avenues. This turn of events nearly broke my young heart, but very probably saved my young neck. There was still light at the end of the tunnel, however. If I could successfully complete twenty-five bombing missions, I could reapply for pilot training and that was my new goal.

Chapter 5

REDIRECTION

I was recommended for navigation training and after reclassification procedures by way of Nashville, Tennessee, I was sent for ground school at Ellington Field, just out of Pasadena, Texas. Before I finished that course, however, an urgent call came for volunteers to take bombardier training with the promise of earning a commission a full six weeks earlier. I took this option since I still dreamed of getting back into pilot training as soon as possible. After finishing bombardier ground school I was transferred to Midland, Texas, for bombardier flight training. Stationed at that base was a Lt. Colonel Jack Ryan who directed the program. Cadets ranked the very lowest on every totem pole everywhere and by now figuratively stood two steps to the rear and left of any other personnel. My own dampened ego received an unexpected boost when Colonel Ryan remarked favorably on my running ability and designated me to run with him, along with a couple of his aides, whenever he could spare the time. During the course of the program I learned that he enjoyed cigars and since my dad sent me a box every month, far more than I could ever smoke myself, one day I unobtrusively presented Colonel Ryan with a box of Tampa's best. Twenty years later when he was a five star general, known as Black Jack Ryan, Commander of SAC, Strategic Air Command, our paths briefly crossed once more. I was astounded when he sought me out and presented me with a box of fine cigars!

My training finally complete, I was graduated and received my bombardier wings at the age of twenty, a second lieutenant in the United States Army Air Corps, ready for action. As I was anxiously pondering where the action might take me, my bilingual ability brought a new opportunity my way. I could attend gunnery school, earn a second set of wings, and become a ground school and flight school instructor training Mexican recruits. This program was part of the United States' endeavor to assist Mexico in developing an air force which might then join the Allies in the war effort. If I couldn't be in the pilot's seat, I had no particular desire to spend the war in the air, and if I remained in the U.S. I might be able to re-enter pilot training sooner than if I tried to complete twenty-five missions overseas! I accepted the opportunity.

Cadet Fernandez, Midland, Texas, 1943

Chapter 6

SNAKE BIT!

As part of my revised training program I was sent to gunnery school at a base near Laredo, Texas. The gunnery range was located in an arid, unpopulated area about ten miles from town. Since by noon the heat would be unbearable, we were on line by 5:00 a.m. and finished by 10:00 a.m.

A number of comfort stations had been dug for our use, but we approached them very cautiously as the desert rattlesnakes found the dark, relatively cool pits quite to their liking. We always took the precaution of firing several shots from a forty-five into the cavity, then stood back and dodged as the snakes, fleeing from the odor of gunpowder, boiled out.

One of our new trainees, dutifully warned, made the mistake of peering into the hole as he fired. Proving that no action is without reaction, a backsplash of the outhouse contents caught him. He roared out faster than the snakes, disgustingly chocolate covered! The only remedy for that poor guy was to strip him of his flight suit and douse him with the fire extinguisher!

Chapter 7

FIRE POWER!

Some excitement came to Laredo with the arrival of the famous Emerson Turret. The turret, which had proved itself on the B-24 Liberator Bomber, was to undergo remodeling with additional firepower. Two 50 caliber machine guns were added, making a total of four and a 37mm cannon was installed. The call went out for volunteers, compact types, to test these improvements and I was selected.

The turret was mounted on a flatbed truck which was driven on a raised embankment. The target was pulled along a track in a field off to the right. Combat conditions were to be simulated and I was required to don all regulation flight gear. That stipulation saved my life. The turret was a tight fit, even for a small guy, and I actually had to chin myself to swing my legs into the turret pit. I closed and latched the doors behind me and took hold of the controls which were like motorcycle handlebars and operated much the same way to turn the turret right or left, up or down. The command was given to commence firing as the truck and target began moving. I was directed to begin with one 50 caliber gun, add the second, then the third, and then to fire all four at once. When I had all that going, the command came to superadd the cannon. When I pressed that button, the blast was all I was aware of until I regained consciousness and found myself in a ditch. The force of all that firepower at once had blown me right through the turret doors and off the flatbed truck to tumble head over heels into the ditch left from building the embankment.

When I did regain consciousness I found myself surrounded by personnel who were prodding and poking me, no doubt to determine the extent of my injuries. I remember my strongest emotion at the time was anger, and I shouted at them to go away and let me alone. They took me to a field house and then to the base hospital where examination proved that I suffered only considerable bruising and a mild concussion. I was issued a three-day pass. That was the last I ever heard of the Emerson Turret and to this day I know not what became of it!

Chapter 8

FRESH SALMON AND DEAD PIGS

I did earn my gunnery wings, but the grand plan to train Mexican airmen was never actualized and once again I found myself awaiting my combat assignment. I wanted B-17s and this time my hopes were realized. I was assigned to Moses Lake Army Air Base in Washington and there our crew was formed.

The climate and landscape features of the state of Washington were quite different from what I was used to, growing up in Florida. The scenery was beautiful and I found the residents to be friendly and supportive. I enjoyed my short term there and especially remember one three-day pass. Four of my buddies and I spent a day and night in bustling Seattle, where, as a consequence of so many soldiers and even more sailors, the bars were hopping. There was a saying around that if a man was tossed out of a bar and rolled across the street, he would just roll into another bar! We went sight-seeing and bought souvenirs. The next day we visited one of the Indian reservations. Indians were subjected to many forms of discrimination during that time in history, but nevertheless they welcomed us warmly, especially, I believe, because we arrived with a bottle of whiskey which they were prohibited from buying. We traded the spirits for a day's salmon fishing and filled our motor pool vehicle without ever baiting a hook. The salmon were running so closely packed that we had only to jab with a pitchfork and toss them into the truck. That evening the mess hall served fresh fish!

From Moses Lake we went on to Sioux City, Iowa, to practice bombing runs from a B-17, using hundred pound bombs filled with sand. The targets were mapped and marked out in unpopulated areas of the Iowa countryside and often difficult to spot. Our initial passes documented the need for this practice and we had our frustrations! Since credit was not given for an uncompleted bomb run, no one wanted to return to the base with bombs on board. If the target was not identified the bombs might be "salvoed," our term for unloading them into the river. Unfortunately, they did not always hit where we intended. One day a very angry looking farmer drove his pickup to the base and demanded to see the Base Commander. The following day a directive was issued banning salvos. That farmer's truck, we learned, was full of sand covered dead pigs!

After final crew training at Sioux City, Iowa, we went to Grand Island, Nebraska, to pick up our brand new silver B-17, among the first to head into combat without camouflage. We set out for our overseas base by way of Maine, Newfoundland and Scotland, and finally arrived at Glatton, England.

B-17 Flying Fortress

Chapter 9
PRACTICING FOR THE REAL THING

At Glatton we began our practice bombing runs. With near a hundred airfields in that area of Great Britain our training runs were conducted in relatively narrow corridors. We needed to become smoothly proficient with pre-flight, take-off and landing procedures, and in the air, regrouping, falling out of formation and re-entering, climbing out, and especially flying in tight formation. As we became more skilled in these operations, our runs took on the semblance of actual raids, and we flew farther and farther on the route we would eventually take into Germany.

The enemy never knew when one of these flights might become an actual raid, but they were ready for us. German espionage was quite efficient and impressive. They seemed to know where we were at all times. We often tuned our radios to the German propaganda stations featuring the notorious, American-born, Nazi propaganda broadcaster, "Axis Sally," because she always had the latest intelligence reports, slanted though they were, and played popular American music, providing a little pleasant nostalgia, but then she would goad us by revealing that she knew when we took off, from where, and the number of aircraft in the flight.

"Come on in, Bomber Boys," she would seductively coo. "We have a welcoming committee waiting for you. Don't expect to see your comrades again in this war!" She tried hard to demoralize us, but instead her broadcasts had the opposite effect. We were champing at the bit to get into the fight.

Chapter 10

CONNECTING

My brother, Frank, was serving with the infantry in New Guinea, but my brother, Ferdie, attached to Intelligence at High Wycombe, was close enough to visit, and whenever we were granted respite from training, I tried to see him. I would remove my gas mask from its case, a real no-no, throw in a clean shirt, a change of underwear and clean socks, catch the train to London Station, take the "tube" to the outskirts of the city and a tram to the base.

On my first visit Ferdie secured a room for us on the third floor of a small London hotel intending to show me some of the "in" places of the city. We were relaxing in our room, discussing plans for the evening, when the air raid siren sounded. By this time Londoners had become rather blasé about these raids and calmly took whatever precautions they thought appropriate. The nearest shelter was some distance from us so we just stayed put. Unfortunately, a bomb hit nearby causing our building to collapse. My brother and I stepped out of our third floor window directly onto the rubble filled street. We purchased some fish and chips, served in newspaper, from a sidewalk vendor who had not even suspended his operation, sat down on the curb and enjoyed our snack. Luckily, notwithstanding the collapse of the hotel, no one there suffered more than minor injuries.

The next time I had an opportunity to see Ferdie I didn't reach the base gate until 2:00 a.m. Security was very tight and the guards had to verify that I was indeed stationed at Glatton and that I did indeed have a brother at this location. By the time verification was accomplished, the Officers' Club employees on the morning shift were arriving and kindly suggested I accompany them to the club where I could wait in relative warmth and comfort. I found my way to a room with a huge fireplace at one end, took off my shoes, curled up in a large easy chair and fell sound asleep. I awoke to a cacophony of strident voices and saw several British officers who ordered me to stand and raise my arms. I attempted to put on my shoes, but they were in the hands of one of the officers who seemed to be examining them quite closely. Another of the officers was probing my gas mask case and demanding an explanation of its unusual contents. Two more officers took turns thoroughly patting me down. They withdrew to confer, and I'm sure I heard some muffled laughter as they considered my obvious stupefaction. One from the group courteously returned my shoes and apologized for the rough handling, assuring me that maintaining unbreached security was their paramount concern.

Chapter 11

THE REAL THING

No matter how many simulated bombing runs we made, nothing could prepare us for the real event. Our initiation came on February 21, 1944. Pre-flight alone was a hard day's work. After an early morning officers' briefing and quick breakfast, we met the rest of our flight crew and ground crew at the aircraft. My responsibility was to inspect and supervise the gunners in addition to my main concern, the loading of the bombs. A rookie gunner, replacing one of the regular men, reported to me, gave a snappy salute and called me "Sir." As I returned the salute, looking at a kid of about seventeen, I realized that I, at age twenty, was considered an old hand! I got him squared away and turned my attention to the bombs.

A delivery truck drove up to the airstrip and disgorged ten 500 pound bombs onto the runway. The ground crew then used pulleys to bring them under the open bomb bay and load them on board. An improperly positioned bomb could, and occasionally would, fall back out onto the concrete below. Only after they were all safely in place did I attach the nose and tail fuses.

Even though the weather was quite cold, after a couple of hours of labor my clothing was damp from perspiration. I quickly stripped off the damp and changed into something dry because at altitude sweat could freeze. Although everyone who ever flew in a B-17 had tremendous respect for that airplane, sometimes bordering on affection, it certainly boasted no amenities. It had no heat, so when we were garbed for the sub-zero temperature encountered at altitude, we could barely move! I wore three pairs of socks inside fleece lined boots, long johns under a blue "bunny" suit which could be plugged into the electrical system for heating, and over that my flight suit. On my hands I wore silk gloves under fleece lined leather ones. My head was covered by a soft, fleece lined helmet. When we got close to enemy territory, I would add a flak jacket, a flak helmet and when the flak got heavy, an infantryman's metal helmet. Along with all of that I wore goggles, an oxygen mask and a parachute harness.

Now I turned my attention to flak-proofing, as best I could, my domain in the nose section. I laid out my reserve ammunition belts and over them I spread a couple of extra flak jackets I had appropriated for this purpose. I had seen enough evidence of the power of flak to pierce an aircraft from any angle, but most often from bottom to top, to make me very conscious of the vulnerability of my relatively unprotected rear end.

Finally the command was given to start engines. Starting an engine could not be done with a simple flick of the pilot's wrist but required the power provided from an auxiliary power unit or "putt-putt" as we called it. Every plane carried one which was cranked up and then provided the juice to start engine number one. Once the first engine was going, the others could be started in rotation.

At last, our aircraft, loaded with 5,000 pounds of bombs, 18,000 plus pounds of fuel, 2,000 pounds of men in flight gear, thousands of rounds of ammunition and everything else needed, was ready to roll. Take-off in a mission ready B-17 was always tense. We all had witnessed, more than once, planes which could not get airborne crash at the end of the runway. Mid-air collisions, with thousands of planes in a foggy sky, were also a definite danger. If you spotted another plane close to yours, it was too late for any evasive action. You just had to hope the trajectory would take it past you.

From the moment our sleek, silver bird began to taxi, my heart was in my throat and beating furiously. Our flight took off at dawn in dense fog at sixty second intervals. When we broke through the fog, planes were scattered for miles in all directions. We re-formed and headed toward the group leader who had fired flares to direct us. As usual, the Channel was blanketed with fog as we began our flight toward the enemy coast.

My position was forward of the pilots' armor plated compartment, in the Plexiglas nose with a gun on either side of me and two guns in the remote controlled chin turret below. The first sight of enemy action appeared in the distance as black, deadly thunderclouds of flak which darkened the sky above the fog. Our target was several hundred miles into Germany. We held our course as best we could while our plane spasmed from shock waves and flak hits. At, "Bombs away!" the plane, delivered of its payload, leaped upward. Our pilot had to avoid other planes engaged in the same macabre ballet, while climbing as rapidly as possible. Simultaneously our guns went into action battling the defending Messerschmits and Focke-Wulfs. Not carrying camouflage paint gave us greater speed and range, but we glinted like new nickels in the sun and were clear targets. We could see other planes explode in mid-air or wheel over, trailing smoke, and spiral into the ground. We anxiously watched for parachutes and if we saw them felt relieved, but sometimes there were none. We made it back to our base with sixty-three flak holes, half a tail and two noncritical casualties. We counted ourselves lucky.

Daylight raids were murder, our bombers knocked out of the sky in alarming numbers. On a raid to Schweinfurt, deep into enemy territory, the carnage was terrible. Schweinfurt, a ball bearing production center, was desperately defended with heavy flak from below and German fighters attacking from all sides. An AA 105, the most powerful German anti-aircraft shell, pierced our plane from bottom to top just between the bomb bay and the radio operator. The waist gunner was not so lucky. Shrapnel slashed his hip and broke his arm leaving bone protruding. I broke out three of the prepared morphine syringes, got my fingers into a tear in his flight suit, ripped it open enough to find leg muscle, shot him up and applied pressure to stanch the blood.

Now there came a call from the ball turret gunner. The spinning and swaying of his position had triggered severe motion sickness. "I've got to get out of here," he yelled. "I'm going to vomit!" I was the only other crew member small enough to get into the ball turret so we quickly traded places. I curled into position with my feet higher than my head and my line of sight between my legs. The ball turret was the most vulnerable gun position but at the same time the widest ranging with the ability to turn 360 degrees. There were automatic "stops" on the guns so that in the heat of battle it wasn't possible accidentally to shoot our own propellers. It was a wild ride! I felt like I was in a shooting gallery and for me it was exhilarating. Once more we made it back to our base to fight again another day. After that raid I gave everything of value I owned to Ferdie. I was beginning to doubt my immortality.

On a mission

Enemy flak

The famous "Flak Dodger"

Chapter 12

A CLOSE CALL

A couple of mornings later I was in Base Operations, taking care of whatever business had brought me there, when I was commandeered by the Ops Officer, "Fernandez! Get your gear. You're on a crew to Beachy Head leaving in twenty minutes." There was no argument allowed here, so I grabbed just my basic gear and got on board. We were flying a minimum crew on a stripped down B-17 used for noncombat missions. This time we were to pick up rescued airmen from a plane that had ditched (crash landed) in the Channel. The weather that morning was foul, as usual, a day good only for seagulls. There was no landing strip at our destination, but that was no problem for the British. They had developed portable metal mesh mats that could be laid down almost anywhere. We landed, taxied around, picked up the survivors and took off immediately. Our radio contact gave us a different heading on the return trip, north around Southampton. Suddenly we realized we were in the middle of a barrage balloon defense area! Barrage balloon fields were disastrous to aircraft. The cables could shear off a wing like a hot knife through butter! There was no way out of this routing error, so we collectively held our breath for what seemed an eternity until we finally heard, "You're clear! Take your heading for Glatton."

Our passengers were never aware of their close call, but I couldn't help thinking, "What a way to go—cut down by our own team's defenses!"

Back at Base Ops, the duty officer said, "Fernandez, you're a bombardier. You weren't supposed to be on this flight."

I could only reply, "Now you tell me!"

Chapter 13

THE FIRST TO BOMB BERLIN!

What I expected to be a routine raid brought surprising consequences. I was a replacement bombardier on a crew that was part of a group with orders to take off over the North Sea, cross Norway, come around south into Germany and deliver bombs on a particular target. If weather or other conditions interfered, we were to bomb a "target of opportunity." We surmised that we were mainly a diversionary group to draw enemy planes away from the main raid which would be the long awaited first American raid on Berlin. The date was March 3rd, 1944. Weather conditions were extremely poor and only worsened, with thunderheads still boiling above 32,000 feet. Visibility was dangerously limited and mid-air collisions a real hazard. We later learned that most of the bombers in our group had returned to Base because of the unusually bad weather, but our crew plowed on. As we turned south and descended to bombing altitude, a few ragged holes appeared in the clouds and a visual fix told us we were crossing the German coast about forty or fifty miles north of Berlin. We could see no other planes from our group, so we joined up with a group of B-17s apparently heading for Berlin. Our "target of opportunity" became the German capital. Having successfully carried out our orders, we headed back to Glatton feeling quite pleased with ourselves. As we approached the landing strip we could see a group of officers awaiting us. We dared to imagine that we would be receiving commendations for being among the first Americans to bomb Berlin. However, as soon as we landed and scrambled out, we faced what appeared to be a strangely "unwelcoming" committee. We were escorted to a waiting bus where we were required to surrender our weapons. Obviously there was a significant problem, but we were completely bewildered as to what it might be. Our uncommunicative escort delivered us to a Quonset hut furnished with tables and stools, posted a guard outside the front and rear doors, left a monitor in the hut and provided us with coffee and sandwiches. We were cautioned not to converse with one another, but that couldn't keep us from guardedly conjecturing about what might be wrong. We had no clue. I happened to have a crank telephone in my B-4 bag and, noticing an outlet in a corner, gathered what appeared to be a casual group around me and tried to call Ferdie since he was attached to Intelligence at High Wycombe and I thought he might know what our problem could be.

As he was a sergeant, I had to go through several operators until, finally, after thirty or forty anxious minutes, I got to him and explained the situation as best I could. His immediate response was to ask, "You didn't bomb Berlin—did you?"

"We certainly did," I replied, "and we have the pictures to prove it!"

"Holy—!" he burst out. "I'll get back to you." Although I had great confidence in Ferdie, I knew he could never get back to an isolated Quonset hut at Glatton.

Now the debriefings began. We were questioned about every detail of our flight, but the main thrust of the interrogation concerned radio communications. The radio operator was asked if he had relayed the mission recall order to the pilot. Since we were not part of the actual

Berlin raid, we had received no such recall order. Not satisfied with this, we were asked which of us had made the decision to ignore the recall order. Of course, not having received any such order, no one could have been guilty of ignoring it. Our interrogators continued to snipe at us, seemingly trying to catch one of us in a lie. We were a group of offended and angry young airmen. The unfairness and accusatory tone of the continuing inquisition so incensed me that my indignation boiled over. Heedless of possible repercussions I called the colonel in charge a pencil pusher! I told him he could benefit from a dose of reality and suggested that he assign himself the experience of a real bombing mission!

We were finally released to our quarters with the admonition not to discuss the matter. This admonition we did ignore. We deduced that the B-17s we had joined on their way to Berlin were part of a major raid that had been recalled. We felt that actually getting through to bomb Berlin was a heroic deed. We had been jubilant upon our return, expecting to be congratulated and commended, but instead had been arrested! Evidently our small contribution, for which we had risked our lives, only served to dilute the great "Sunday Punch" raid planned by General

Doolittle. My heated outburst did bring consequences although not what I might have expected. I was issued a three-day pass with orders to cool down!

Within a week that same B-17, with the regular crew on board, was rammed in mid-air by a German fighter. There were no survivors.

Following the Berlin raid I completed two more missions. The next one brought a particularly nasty surprise. We were expecting to run the usual, brutal gamut, but suddenly thunderous explosions split the air causing our B-17 to buck and shudder to shouts of, "What the *** was that!" "That" was the detonation of German rockets launched from German jet aircraft into our bomber formation, a staggering revelation of what lay in store if the enemy were allowed to perfect such new instruments of destruction.

Chapter 14
FATE STEPS IN

Once again my fate was altered by a freak accident. Since I had undergone special gunnery training, it was my responsibility to inspect our fifty caliber machines guns to ensure that the gunners were properly cleaning them with oil and thoroughly drying them. The weather in March at Glatton was extremely cold and although gun oil was to be rigorously accounted for, from time to time the men would take along a half empty can to energize the coke fire in their potbelly stoves. After observing that the cleaning was progressing satisfactorily on this particular occasion, I left the gunnery hut and stepped into the adjacent Quonset hut for some purpose. It was frigid in there and as I saw that the fire in the stove seemed to be in danger of flickering out I lifted the lid and stoked the coke embers, never suspecting that a can of oil, thoughtlessly tossed into the stove, had reached flash point. The oil caught and flame erupted, searing my face and blinding me! My shouts brought two airmen who quickly commandeered three bicycles, put me on the middle one and with each of them holding one of my handlebars guided while we all peddled until we came upon a vehicle which could take me the rest of the way to the base hospital.

After two days my vision improved enough that I could get around and I was issued a three-day pass. I went to Bury-St-Edmunds to visit a hometown friend stationed there, with the intention of proceeding to High Wycombe the following day to spend some time with Ferdie. That evening, just as I was preparing to retire at the local Red Cross billeting shelter there came a knock at my door. I opened it to two MPs, Military Policemen, who, determining that I was Lt. Augustine Fernandez of the 457th Bomb Group, informed me that I must immediately return to Base. My pass did not stipulate that I was on leave for medical reasons, and notwithstanding a blistered face lacking eyebrows or lashes, the administrative officer in charge cleared me for active duty. I was delivered back to the base at Glatton and dropped off on the flight line. I expected to be able to return to my quarters for my flight gear, but departure time did not allow that. I downed a couple of hard English biscuits and a cup of coffee, all that was available on the flight line. I was inserted into a crew whose regular bombardier was on medical leave for stress related problems. The navigator, "Mark" Markowitz, had extra gear on the flight line and I was directed to use it. When I was picked up I was wearing my dress "pinks," as we called them, and still wearing that uniform I slipped into Markowitz' extra flight gear and hurriedly prepared for departure. I did not know that Mark had sewn one of his dog tags into the lining of the "escape and evade" jacket that I was wearing. The date was March 29, 1944.

Our pilot, Lew Lennartson, had had his share of misfortunes on prior missions. Returning from a mission earlier in the month he had tried to coax his damaged plane back to Base but couldn't make it, ditching in the frigid Channel. The crew was rescued and most returned to duty. On his next mission the aircraft developed engine trouble and he was forced to abort. Lew's flight history had no meaning for me until I happened to overhear a ranking officer tell him that failure to complete this mission was not acceptable, and if he should abort, he would sit out the rest of the war in the co-pilot's seat. I remember thinking at the time that such an admonition was highly uncalled for.

The B-17 we drew that morning had a record of mechanical problems on a previous foray resulting in the loss of one engine, forcing a return to Base. On this morning, however, everything was running smoothly as we took off, joined our flight and headed for the enemy coast. In addition to Lennartson and Markowitz, the other crew members that day were Mike Keesee, co-pilot, Tom Haag, flight engineer, Joe Fontaine, ball turret gunner, William Graham, radio operator, Clyde Garnhart and Gilbert Goode, waist gunners and "Blackie" Blackwell, tail gunner.

When we were about ninety miles from the industrial targets of Brunswick, misfortune hit. The number one engine failed. We might have dumped the payload and tried to make it back to Base by flying on the deck, but Lew decided that the better part of valor was to continue the raid. At, "Bombs away!" we made our precipitous climb but did not have the power to pull back into formation. As we veered off we became an immediate easy target for the wolf pack of Messerschmits and Focke-Wulfs.

My words today cannot begin to convey the chaos and emotions of those last minutes. All hell broke loose! Four German fighters came down on us at once sweeping in from all directions. Tom yelled to me from the top turret, "He's coming in from 2 o'clock—get him at 10!" Enemy strafing riddled us causing extensive damage to the fuselage and blowing up engine number two. Suddenly I realized that my guns in the nose were the only ones firing—all the other guns or gunners had been knocked out! I saw a Focke-Wulf boldly coming in from the side, so close I could see the pilot looking us over. He no doubt thought himself quite safe, unaware that my chin turret guns could swivel a hundred eighty degrees. I turned those guns on him and blew him out of the sky!

The only access to the cockpit from the nose was a crawlway which I scrambled up as fast as I could. As I passed Mark I noticed he had not moved from his position and seemed frozen in a state of shock. Tom was in the cockpit area and appeared to be uninjured, so I popped open my mask and yelled that I was going to the rear of the plane to answer calls for help from there. I sucked in a lungful of oxygen, dropped the bottle, and holding my breath, clambered through the bomb bay to the back of the aircraft where I hooked up to another bottle before anoxia, the euphoria of oxygen deprivation, could catch me. Blood was everywhere! Both waist gunners had been hit and were obviously in agonizing pain. Removing flight gear and clothing at 40 below zero to treat wounds would have been sheer folly, so I pulled off a glove and shouted at Graham to toss me a morphine pack. He did so, but in my agitated haste, I dropped it. He tossed me two more and I was able to inject both men. The ball turret was completely shattered and Joe apparently dead of massive injuries. We tried to work out some way to retrieve him, but it was hopeless! If he had somehow miraculously survived, there could be no getting out. I released the rear door, and we shoved out the auxiliary power unit, the machine guns, ammo belts and anything else that would lessen the weight of the aircraft. Then I ordered the men to bail out! Back in the cockpit area, I saw that Lew and Mike were both seriously wounded, but Lew refused to leave the controls, trying to hold the airplane from going into a fatal spin until everyone else was out. Mike's injuries included a broken leg and he could not extricate himself from his seat. Tom got him up, helped him to the open bomb bay, pushed him out and tried to take over the co-pilot controls, but Lew ordered him, "Get out, now!"

"Lew!" I shouted. "We're going down! Goddammit! We're going down! Now!" I saw that he was wounded and hollered, "Haag! Help me! Help me get him out!" But Lew wouldn't allow it. He adamantly refused to leave. I went back for Mark, who still hadn't moved, pulled him up and shoved him ahead of me into the cockpit. I suddenly realized that I didn't have my parachute pack! It was back in the nose of the plane! And Mark didn't have his either! There were always extras stored around, but could I find them quickly? What would I do if I could find only one? "Let there be two," I prayed, and then I saw them! There were two! I hooked one onto my harness and one onto his, grabbed him and pulled him along to the bomb bay. I pushed him through and followed after him. I could see that he was not going to jump, so I wrapped my arms and my legs around him and we tumbled out in tandem. When I pulled his ripcord, the billowing parachute yanked him from my grasp. Only moments later our plane exploded into a huge fireball. I could feel the force of the blast as I was free-falling away and I knew that two fine men had been lost.

Chapter 15

CAPTURED!

I stayed in my free-fall, to avoid becoming a target, as long as possible, and when my 'chute did open, the ground came up to meet me quickly. I found myself in a plowed field bordered on three sides with forest and on the fourth side a road. I dropped my harness as fast as I could and started running for the trees. I was about halfway there when I spotted a German soldier on a motorbike, carrying a long rifle. He rode onto the field and brought his bike around cutting me off from the woods. I changed direction, but he came around and cut off my escape again. After the third try, my legs could run no farther. My "moment of truth" was upon me. To submit went against everything I thought I represented. I could shoot this fellow and make an attempt to find my way in my American flight uniform back to Allied territory, but that plan was truly foolhardy. I tossed my gun parts as far as I could in different directions, stood still and raised my hands in surrender. My captor motioned me to proceed along the road as he wheeled his bike behind me. We soon came to a small village and were met by a group that appeared to be town officials. A crowd of civilians also had gathered and were shouting in very menacing tones. We had been warned not to surrender to civilians as they had no qualms about taking justice into their own hands with whatever weapons were available, including pitchforks, and even burning captives alive, the fate I dreaded most. I figured it was at least a little lucky that I was captured by the military but I could not escape the civilian fury. Every chance they got they pressed in on me. They did manage to get hold of me and I was dragged along the road as they kicked, cuffed, and battered me with whatever they had that could be used as a weapon. I was taken to a barn, emotionally and physically drained, my head swollen and bleeding from scalp lacerations, and locked in for the night. It was miserably damp and cold in the barn, but there was a mound of hay in the stall and I did my best to find a little warmth by burrowing into it. I was exhausted, but with the cold, my anxiety and the commotion going on outside, sleep was out of the question. Later that night another prisoner was brought in. It was Markowitz. He was a bloody mess, hardly recognizable, and far worse off than I was. He obviously had been severely beaten but was silent and did not acknowledge me.

At dawn the doors were opened and two lumps of blood sausage with hunks of coarse black bread were thrown down on the hay stack. Before I could get to my portion, another hand reached for it. I saw that an elderly man had picked it up and was carefully removing pieces of straw from the sausage. After he had done so, he placed it on his handkerchief and offered it to me. Since I knew I deserved no pity from my captors and expected none, his gesture, recognizing our mutual human brotherhood, was especially moving. I ate my share of the food and was glad to get it, but noticed that Mark did not touch his.

Some time later we were taken from the barn to the town square and held there. I did not see what happened to Mark and I dreaded to imagine what might be in store for him. I was driven to some fairly large town where later that day two officers from the feared Schutzstaffel, or SS, (Nazi Elite Guard) showed up. I kept my eyes on the ground, avoiding eye contact, but there was no mistaking those snappy black uniforms ending in glossy black boots. My peripheral vision also noticed a couple of green uniforms and I knew that army personnel had arrived. I was thoroughly searched and Mark's dog tag was revealed. The two officers then began loudly arguing about me. I heard one word I did know, *"Jude,"* Jew, and I knew they must have found something identifying me as Markowitz. That added another layer of anxiety to my predicament. Before the army officers could take any action, however, Luftwaffe (air force) personnel arrived, claimed me, and I heard for the first time those famous, daunting words, "For you the war is over!"

In the custody of two Germans I was put aboard a train packed with prisoners. I spotted Tom Haag standing in the crowd at the opposite end of the car but we made no signs of recognition. Sometime later the train pulled into a station and I was taken off. While we awaited further transportation my captors shackled me to a bench and took themselves to a nearby tavern leaving me to become fair game for a pair of teenagers who happened along and helped themselves to my boots and socks. My feet began to burn as frostbite set in and soon were completely numb. About then I noticed that an old woman bundled in layers of shawls and scarves had stopped and bent over near my feet. At first I wasn't aware of what she was doing, but then I realized that she had pulled off two of her scarves and bound up my bare feet. I was again confounded by such kindness towards an enemy who had very recently been dropping death on the "fatherland." She exemplified the true meaning of the word "charity" and I have never forgotten her.

Chapter 16
INTERROGATION

When we finally reached the Dulag Luft, the interrogation center, in Oberusel just northwest of Frankfurt, I was checked over by International Red Cross staff. They provided me with a jacket, boots two sizes too large, socks and a small kit containing soap and a toothbrush. The first time I was taken out of my cell the toothbrush disappeared. I later learned that a toothbrush was a real prize and quite valuable on the cigarette driven POW market.

Now my solitary incarceration began. I was confined to a space about six by twelve feet with a naked light bulb and a heater in the ceiling and a small barred air shaft in the wall, too high for anyone to reach. The cell door was solid metal with a small slot for checking on the inmate. There was nothing in my cell except a small cot attached to the wall, a hard mat and a thin blanket. The only other amenity was a tin can to be used for waste, but nothing was provided for cleaning oneself and I had to tear off small squares of my "pink" dress uniform shirt to serve as toilet paper. I had so little to eat, however, thin soup and black bread, that bodily functions required a piece of my shirt only two or three times a week. A guard did take me out of my cell once to a regular bathroom. I noticed a shower stall, turned the water on and ducked my head under. It felt great, but I was alarmed to see that the water running off was quite red. I gingerly explored my scalp which was still swollen and very sore, but I didn't find any open wounds.

It was not possible to tell night from day and I eventually lost track of time. The light bulb would be turned on for a period and then off, without any set schedule. When the heater in the ceiling was operating it gave out such intense heat that I would soon find it difficult to breathe and have to strip off my sweat soaked clothes. Then the heater would be turned off and I would put on everything I had, wrap myself in the thin blanket and curl up, shivering, on the cot. A guard came by about every hour day and night to peer through the slot and kick the door. Just when I thought I had the timing down and a kick on the door was coming, there would be none, an hour was skipped. Rest was impossible.

After three or four days, the cell door was opened and two guards appeared. One of them motioned to me and said, "*Kommen Sie mit.*" (Come.) They took me down a long corridor with one stop to use a bathroom and splash some water on my face. With a week's worth of stubble on my chin, no chance for personal hygiene, ill fitting, mismatched clothes and my Charlie Chaplin boots, I was ushered into an office which was elegant yet precisely military. The furniture was luxurious; there were pictures and swastikas on the walls and plush drapes at the windows. Behind an impressive desk sat the enemy, a young, smartly attired German officer just oozing self-assurance and control. He finished what he appeared to be reading, looked up at me and said, in perfect, unaccented English, "Ah, Lieutenant Fernandez, please, take a seat." When I silently remained standing, he proceeded to tell me all about myself. I have to admit I was quite surprised at the extent of his knowledge. He knew my parents were immigrants from Spain, that I had two brothers and where they were serving, where I took my training and where I was based. To every question he put to me I steadfastly responded with my name, rank and serial number. We were ordered, if captured, to respond in this way for the first five days of captivity. After that span of time, anything we might know would have become irrelevant.

I was not interrogated every day, and never by the same person. My final interrogator spoke perfect Spanish and addressed me in that language. He remarked how beautiful northern Spain was, evidently aware that my folks came from that part of the country, and said that he would like to revisit that area sometime in the future. This time I did respond. I told him that if he could get me over the border to Spain a considerable ransom could be his. He looked at me without a word for what seemed a long time and then dismissed me.

Chapter 17

A KICK IN THE PANTS!

Some days later I was removed from my cell and taken to a fenced area where a number of other prisoners were gathered. Our guard was a German soldier wearing an overcoat down to his ankles and a helmet and carrying a long rifle. One from our group of prisoners, a Royal Air Force Spitfire pilot, was leaning against the wall with his foot propped up, casually smoking a cigarette in the inimitable British manner, holding it between thumb and index finger. When it was down to a nub, he off-handedly flicked it to the ground behind the guard. I guess even a shred of real tobacco was a prize, for the guard turned around and bent over to retrieve it. The RAF officer uncurled himself, cocked his foot and planted a solid blow to the guard's rear sending him sprawling, his helmet flying in one direction and his rifle in another! Suddenly guards were everywhere, gesticulating, shouting, pointing rifles, demanding that the culprit be identified and threatening to shoot everyone unless the offender was named! I tried to make myself as inconspicuous as possible but I was sure we were goners. No one ratted. Everyone remained motionless, eyes on the ground. Gradually the hubbub subsided. We were warned that any of us who ever touched a guard again would summarily be shot. No one was shot this time, however, and the fact that we were spared retribution planted a small seed of suspicion in my mind. I looked askance at the guilty one, whose name I learned later was Brande, and I wondered.

Chapter 18
STALAG LUFT 1

We were bused to the Frankfurt train station and loaded into wooden boxcars to begin the journey to our permanent prison camp. So many prisoners were packed into one car that it was impossible to sit or lie down; we could only lean against the side of the car or each other. We ached to disembark just to stretch our legs and walk around and the guards were authorized to allow it, but conditions often denied us even this relief. There was nothing in these boxcars but sawdust or sometimes some hay along with two large tin cans for waste. The cans had to be emptied out through a small window with care not to hit a patrolling guard. This was probably the only time I was thankful I was short, too short for that job.

Twice a day the doors slid back and we lined up for our food ration, the same soup and piece of coarse black bread. There was also a barrel of sauerkraut, and we were allowed a fistful if we obeyed the stern warning to shake twice in order to dislodge any kraut sticking to the hand. Since my hands are not large, I tried to get away without shaking. A sudden, sharp rap on my knuckles forced me to drop all my kraut! I couldn't move, frozen by the shock of such a loss. Unexpectedly, the guard gave me a second chance. I grabbed as much sauerkraut as I could but vigorously shook my fist twice—lesson learned! The bread slices were not uniform and the slice that luck brought was a either a daily highlight or a disappointment. We pitied the poor guy who happened to get the thin heel, but whenever someone who was really bad off got the heel those of us in better shape would share with him. A couple of times there was some accounting mix-up and our car would be fed a second round. When that happened we felt like we had hit the jackpot.

As often as I could I positioned myself near Brande, to listen to his conversation. His main theme was how much he hated the Germans. Not only did I believe he protested too much, but I was sure that I detected a German accent to his speech! More and more I suspected a plant.

Prisoner transport was obviously not a priority as our boxcar was often shunted into a yard where we might remain for days at a time until we were picked up again. Locomotives were major objectives of Allied strafing runs, and since prisoner filled boxcars were never marked as such, we were as helpless as sitting ducks. Many men did lose their lives in this way, as accidental targets. I was lucky. I sweated out many a strafing, but my car was never hit. When we reached Berlin we sat on a siding for several days. One of those days stands out vividly in my memory. We heard the sound of approaching aircraft which grew to a thundering roar and then—explosions! The Allies were bombing Berlin! Our boxcar was unguarded, but we were locked in and if an incendiary bomb should hit close enough to ignite it we would be left to burn. After several tense hours the bombing stopped. The next day our boxcar was picked up and we began to move again. By now some of the guys were becoming weak and ill, the worst affliction being diarrhea. Those poor unfortunates stayed at one end of the car with both waste cans and nothing but a little straw for cleanup. The stink was awful, but the least of our worries.

There was much speculation among us as to our destination and when we finally arrived we found ourselves on the outskirts of Barth. We were a dirty, disheveled group when we piled out of the boxcars into the freezing cold to begin the long trek to prison. I saw some Russian prisoners there, apparently to help move the wounded. No one was wounded in our group, but some were too weak to walk. They were loaded onto horse carts and those of us who could took turns pushing them. This sorry band was paraded through the city of Barth and under a handsome arch in the middle of town. Most of the adults along the way pointedly turned their backs to us. A few vented their hatred shouting epithets such as *"Terrefliger"* (terror flier) at us. Some of the children, beautiful, rosy cheeked, angelic looking children, would dart away from their parents, run toward us and pelt us with sharp rocks.

I don't know how far we actually straggled along, but it seemed like many miles before we could see, looming ahead, the daunting, dreary and depressing fences, towers and buildings of Stalag Luft 1. The compound was girded by two tall barbed wire fences, the space between them filled with coiled barbed wire. Watchtowers with spotlights and guards manning machine guns were spaced around outside the fences. Approximately ten feet from the inner fence and running parallel to it was a single strand of wire about two feet from the ground, which, I learned, was the warning wire. Prisoners were commanded not to stray beyond this wire without a guard's permission, or risk being shot.

We were separated into groups with the wounded and ill going one way and the rest of us on to induction. I saw right away that the Russian prisoners had the worst camp duties. We passed a group of them who were pumping out and flushing the nearly overflowing latrine tanks. What a stench!

British airmen were used as medics, and I found myself the object of two of them who had me strip and then attacked me with tongue depressors. I admit I was quite a hairy fellow and they inspected every hair on my body. Their cockney accent was so thick I could barely understand, but one of them said something like, "Thaink the Lawd 'e's cline!"

I realized they meant I was clean and I objected, saying, "No way! I could really use a shower!" They laughed at that and said that being "clean" just meant they had found no lice and I wouldn't have to be shaved from head to toe, a job they wouldn't have relished! I was deloused anyway with a spray of powdered insecticide and sent to Red Cross where I was issued socks, shoes, long john underwear, a shirt, trousers, jacket, cap, gloves, and, lucky me, a scarf. I finally said goodbye to my once nifty but now dirty and tattered, fifty dollar "pink" dress uniform shirt!

We were escorted to the South compound and there was some discussion as to where we should actually be quartered. The barracks housing Americans was full and I was assigned to number 10, with mostly RAF prisoners. We were supplied with a blanket and a burlap bag for a mattress which we had to fill from a mound of wood shavings. The British airmen who were helping us settle in advised us to stuff the bag as full as possible because it would soon flatten out. We were then given five wood slats and assigned a bunk. I got an upper probably because I was strong enough to climb into it.

For me it was a good deal because it was somewhat removed from the hustle-bustle, the comings and goings, of crowded barracks life. Here I heard, for the first time, prisoners referring to themselves as "kriegies" which was how they had shortened the German word, *Kreigsgefangenen*, (prisoner of war).

My first day in camp I, through necessity, became acquainted with the stinking latrines I had smelled when I arrived at the gate. Inside a large barn-like building a long trench had been dug which was covered with planking at seat height. There were two rows of holes back to back with boards down the middle so a man was separated from the man behind him, but not from the person beside him. There were a couple of feet between seats. I saw kriegies with their trousers around their ankles, reading or carrying on conversations with their neighbors, seemingly in no great hurry to leave. I marveled at the self-protective ability of the human psyche because I found that after a few days the stench was hardly noticeable! The Russian *Untermensch*, (sub-humans) as the Germans called them, whom I saw flushing out the vans were also responsible for filling them from the waste in the trenches. They brought a horse drawn cart carrying a tank into the compound, ran a hose into the bottom of the cesspool and set off a charge which created a vacuum drawing the contents into the tank. I don't know where they dumped that load, but rumor had it that human waste was being used to fertilize the fields yielding the vegetables provided to the prisoners.

The barracks were locked down every night, shutters closed, and along with the doors, secured from outside. If a prisoner did not make it into his own barracks before it was locked he would have to dash into any one still open and spend the night on the floor. About an hour after lockdown the barracks lights were extinguished and all was in darkness except for the flashlights of the patrolling guards and the tower searchlights sweeping the grounds. We could peer through cracks in the walls if we wished, but there was usually nothing to see. Strangely enough, now that I was actually in prison camp, I felt safe for the first time since I was captured. I no longer felt in imminent danger of being killed. I was sure we would all be liberated in a few months.

When the barracks door was unlocked in the morning and the shutters opened, the first order of the day was for those designated to rush out for ersatz coffee before the supply ran out. It was awful stuff, but at least it was hot! If there was no coffee on a particular morning, there would, at least, be hot water into which we might shave a little chocolate if we had any.

At the given signal we would fall out for roll call and that, more often than not, required hours depending upon how much guard-baiting the guys were in the mood for. Ducking around and being counted twice was a favorite strategy.

About 9:00 a.m. the Russian prisoners came around trundling huge carts carrying hundreds of loaves of bread which were dumped onto the bare ground. Our group's bread detail would pick up our share of the loaves and just dust them off. That bread was a challenge to chew. I think one of the ingredients was actually sawdust. I know that if I tried to warm it by the stove it would catch fire. In the evenings we got boiled potatoes, maybe some cabbage, bread and hot soup with small pieces of meat in it. Sometimes the vegetables were rutabagas. No matter how hungry I was I just couldn't stomach rutabagas! The meal was skimpy and sometimes showed a little spoilage, but certainly better than I had had for a long time and to me it tasted great! We were always hungry. The guys fantasized more about food than any other aspect of life. My fantasy was my mother's kitchen with pots bubbling on the stove, the air redolent with aromas of her home cooking.

The meager camp rations were supplemented by Red Cross packages which were pooled and shared. Frankly, those packages varied significantly in quality. If they were British, we had powdered milk, corned beef which was pretty tasteless, biscuits as hard as rocks, but great marmalade, chocolate and English cigarettes. The American packages had Spam, powdered KLIM—milk spelled backwards, chocolate, and better cigarettes. Occasionally the packages would include a toothbrush, or a comb, or other small luxury and those would be awarded in a lottery. The odds were pretty steep against winning one. Cigarettes, especially American cigarettes, were strong on the POW trading market. I didn't smoke and was able to trade, but since a toothbrush went for about two hundred American cigarettes, I cleaned my teeth with sand on my index finger. Usually I would trade for chocolate bars.

After a few days I noticed that Brande seemed to visit often in our room. He was tall and seemed considerably older than most of us who were in our early twenties. His voice carried and he was quite talkative. He definitely had a German accent! Again I positioned myself near enough to observe him surreptitiously and analyze his conversation for double agent clues. I told myself that he if proved to be a German agent I would have to kill him, but with what I didn't know! Gradually I came to realize that he was just what he claimed to be, an RAF fighter pilot who was shot down and hated the Germans. He was from South Africa and his accent stemmed from the fact that his primary language was Afrikaans! "Brandy" and I became good friends. He often suffered from what seemed to be quite painful and almost chronic sinus infections. I remember once I found him beating his head against the wall in torment and frustration. The camp certainly had no medicine to spare for what would be considered a minor malady, so during those periods, I did what I could as a friend. He was a smoker and I would share some of my cigarette stash with him. When he was not too bad off, he had many witty stories of his life in South Africa and I came to value and enjoy his company.

My first few weeks in camp I had a hard time adjusting. I found it very difficult to come to terms with the fact that I was really a prisoner, that for me the war was over and I could do nothing more to fight for my country. Probably worst was the realization that I would not finish my twenty-five missions and would not be able call in that promise of re-entering pilot training. I was a thwarted and bitter young man. One day my anger and frustration finally erupted over a frivolous incident. The men in our room did what they could to keep our area reasonably clean and I wanted to help, so I combed the camp grounds for twigs of any size and bundled them together to use as a broom. Sweeping bent over with that "broom" was a pain, but I was new and tried to do my share. One day while Brandy was visiting, he thoughtlessly dropped a cigarette butt on my relatively clean floor and ground it out with his heel. It was a small thing, I know, but it sent me over the edge. To everyone's surprise, I lost it! I went into a rage and ended by telling Brandy that if he ever threw another butt on my floor I would make him pick it up with his lips! He was flabbergasted by my reaction. To his credit he was conciliatory; I apologized, and our friendship weathered the storm.

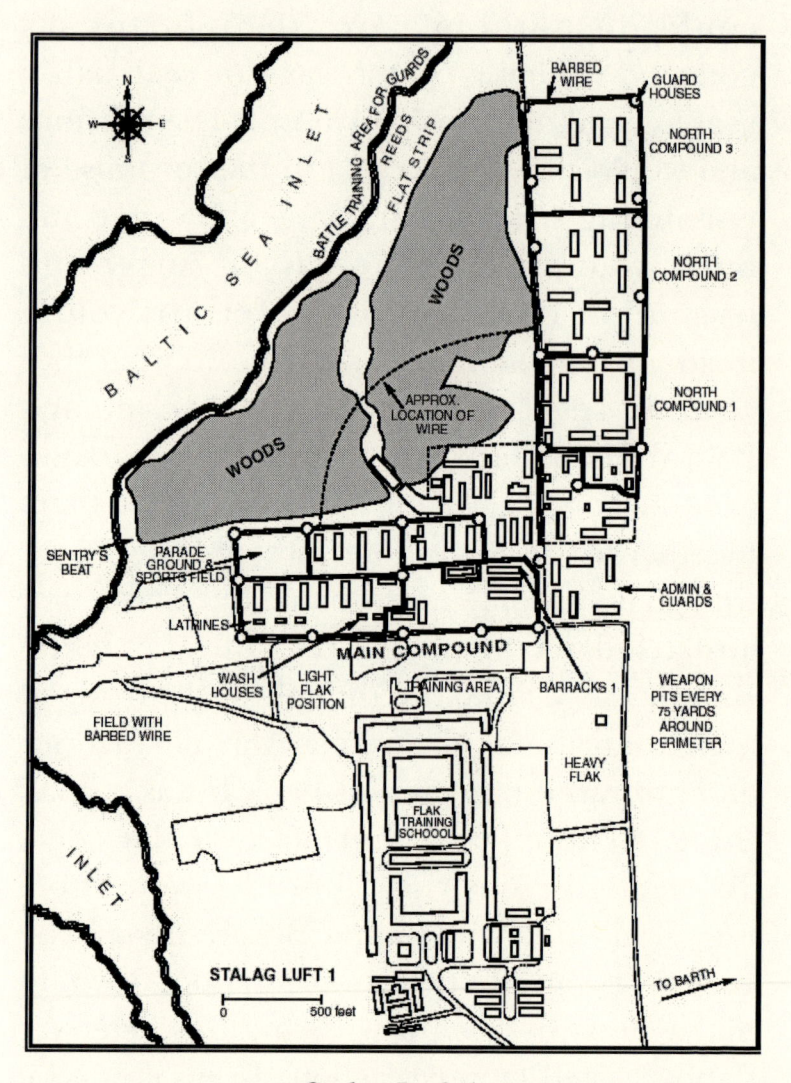

Stalag Luft 1

Fence line and guard tower

Guard tower

German guard

German officer

Preparing to dump bread

Cart full of bread

Unloading potatoes

Potato dump

Red Cross truck

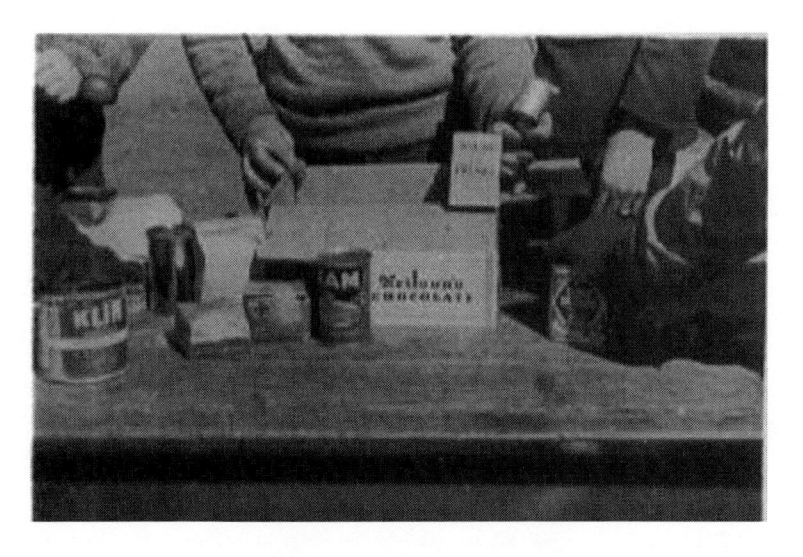

Red Cross package contents

Soccer game

Roll call in winter

Wash house

Frozen laundry

Coke briquettes

Typical stove

Scene from POW play

POWs in female dress

"Das Kooler" Solitary confinement

New arrivals

Chapter 19

ESCAPE SCHEMES

I soon realized that there was much more going on at Stalag Luft 1 than I could have imagined. I often saw groups of men engaged in what seemed to be intense discussions. At first they were secretive, but gradually I was let in on some of the plans. I learned that there were many covert operations afoot, all of which had been submitted to and sanctioned by a screening and evaluation committee. We were encouraged to turn in to the committee any ideas, schemes or escape plans we might devise, but approval was absolutely required so that one project would not inadvertently expose another. Escaping was considered a patriotic duty and many attempts to reach freedom were initiated, especially by the British who seemed to have several diverse projects in the works at all times.

By now I had heard a number of stories about breakout efforts, some quite clever, some briefly successful, others that, to put it kindly, were highly imaginative. One of the more fantastic escape ideas rumored around the camp involved the construction of a catapult made from rubber tubing and a section of tire acquired through bribery and which, when attached to two poles, would vault a ninety pounder, outfitted with civilian clothes, papers and money, right over both fences to liberty. There was more than one volunteer willing to risk landing on his head for a taste of freedom, but saner minds evidently prevailed and this idea never came to fruition.

A variation on that theme called for somehow diverting the attention of the guards while four of the huskier guys took, by his hands and feet, a fellow kriegie completely bundled up in layers of clothing, swung him back and forth to gain momentum and released him to sail over the first fence. He would land on the rolled up barbed wire between the two fences, but the wire would be springy and the clothing would protect him from the vicious spikes. It would be quite difficult to discern a person hiding within the bunched up wire and if he managed to escape detection, then at night he could clip through the outer fence with a prisoner-made pair of wire cutters and be on his way toward the cover of the woods.

The most preposterous design, which might aptly be referred to as a "flight of fancy," was hatched one autumn, before I arrived, when someone noticed that during a storm, or a low ceiling of clouds, a few of the geese migrating south would sometimes get separated from their flight and pass only about fifty feet overhead. The plan was to capture two of those powerful birds and harness them to a skinny kriegie who had canvas covered wings attached to his back. If the birds could get airborne into the fall winds, the kriegie could release them and glide to freedom!

Another scheme which never got past the concept stage called for a docile horse draped with a blanket concealing a kriegie strapped to the animal's belly. The horse, under the charge of a Russian prisoner work gang, would then be led past the guards at the gate. This idea was scrapped because no one could think of any logical reason why a horse would be given a precious kriegie blanket.

The Germans required that every tin can coming into the camp be accounted for. Not only did they puncture all cans so that food could not be stockpiled for escape purposes, but they demanded the return of the empties as they realized that in the hands of ingenious kriegies a tin can could be transformed into many a useful device. A cart was stationed within the camp for cans to be deposited and in the afternoon a horse would be brought in and the cart removed. We knew the guards were not about to count thousands of cans and always kept as many as we thought we could get away with. If the empty cans were found during a search, they were always confiscated. One sharp kriegie saw the cart full of cans as a real opportunity to slip away and almost made it. He climbed into the empty cart, patiently lay there as cans were dumped on top of him and actually did make it through the gate. He remained under that mountain of cans until darkness fell before trying to dig himself out, but then the noise gave him away and he was discovered. After that incident, the guard removing the cart ran his bayonet though the pile of cans before leaving the compound.

One prisoner dressed himself up as a member of a Russian slave labor gang and walked out with them right past the gate. Why anyone would prefer to be part of such a detail I can't imagine. However, when the Russian laborers' count didn't tally, he was returned, after a stay in the cooler, to his barracks.

Enlisted men who according to The Geneva Convention were allowed to be assigned to work details outside the camp took advantage of this provision one day, and shepherded by two other kriegies dressed as German guards boldly marched out of their compound. When they reached the main gate, however, there was no record of any such detail having been scheduled and one more ingenious try was foiled.

The principal thrust of escape efforts centered on tunneling and some prisoners did make it out. The longest period of evasion was something over a month, but no one ever escaped from Stalag Luft I permanently. Upon recapture, a prisoner could expect a stay in solitary with reduced rations.

Chapter 20

OPERATION COOKHOUSE MOLE

I was most eager to be accepted into an escape group, but I understood that I must prove myself to be sensible and cautious and at the same time willing to take risks. My first opportunity came when I was invited to become a "Cookhouse Mole." This operation originated in barracks 11, and a man quartered there traded places with me so that the count would tally in the morning. My small stature was again an asset because getting out of the barracks after lights out was no easy feat. The exit was from the latrine which had two "honey buckets." The floor around one of them had been loosened, and after the honey bucket was lifted out, the floor could be moved just enough for me to squeeze through that noxious opening and land butt first on the ground below. The patrolling sentry with his dog took a usually predictable path, and when he had left our area a signal would come down the line that the coast was clear. We also had a call back signal, a tin can with pebbles in it that was shaken twice. Rattling pebbles meant imminent danger!

I was dressed in dark clothes from head to toe. I had a cap on my head, gloves on my hands and a loose jacket under which I had attached an empty bag for the loot. I waited for the searchlights to finish the sweep over my area and began to worm my way, on my belly, toward the fenced in cookhouse area fifty to sixty yards away. When the searchlight again swept by and over me, I froze, feet flattened out as much as possible, hands beneath my body and my face in the dirt. The light did not pause and I continued toward the fence which appeared to be intact but was not. Previous moles had worked it loose, but after each run, it was semi-secured and the area disguised with dirt. It took several minutes for me to work it loose again and bend it up enough to slip through. My target was the cookhouse garbage dump and my precious booty the potato peels I found there. It was a good night. I filled my bag with peelings, squeezed back through the small opening, carefully reattached and disguised the fence damage and slowly and cautiously wormed my way back. I was greeted by a clap on the shoulder and, "Good job, Fernandez!" I was gratified by the recognition and praise for my efforts. That night I made a second run. The peels were turned over to another committee whose members washed them, cooked them and provided a little extra sustenance to those prisoners in need of it.

Mole runs did not always turn out so successfully. On one occasion after the wriggling and writhing, face in the dirt trip to the dump there were no peels to be had. Another time when the searchlight swept along it stopped right on me. My adrenaline shot up and my heart began to pound. I knew I had to remain absolutely still, but I feared I might not have flattened my feet enough, or perhaps I had moved too fast and stirred up some dust. I realized that if I were to be apprehended, I could be shot or at least my chance to be accepted into an escape group would evaporate. After several agonizing moments, the light continued the sweep. The closest call I experienced came one night when I was about halfway to the fence. Suddenly I heard the rattle of the tin can. I spun around and made my way back as fast as I could, still trying not to make a sound or stir up any dust. When I scrambled back up through the latrine, I learned that the sentry had unexpectedly changed his route and was headed back our way. Altogether over the weeks before I was reassigned to another barracks, I made six mole runs.

The dogs accompanying the guards on their rounds were vicious animals, trained to attack on command. They would be sent to quarter the area beneath a barracks and rejoin the sentry at the other end. Since this could reveal clandestine activities, the prisoners had devised a means to discourage a dog's obedience. It was easy to remove a plank in the floor and let down a wire noose. If a curious dog came near enough to be snagged, he would be strangled to within an inch of his life but never killed, as a dead dog would a mean a dead prisoner. After such an experience, the dog, being no fool, would avoid his master's command and skirt only the edges beneath the barracks.

If the Germans suspected a tunneling operation was underway they would send a man squirming in the dirt under the barracks to search the area and to eavesdrop on conversations, hoping to overhear escape plans. These ferrets, as they were termed, emphasized the impotence of the captives and were thoroughly despised by all.

Chapter 21

I MAKE MYSELF USEFUL

RAF prisoners were the most determinedly escape oriented of all the POWs. No matter how many of their tunnels were discovered they always had one more underway. My courage as a mole had the results I eagerly hoped for. I was given the chance to be a tunnel assistant with my first assignment being that of helper in dirt disposal. Tunnels required the disposition of significant amounts of the nearly white sandy soil, and some very crafty methods had been devised to take care of the problem. Long fabric tubes, like stockings, open at each end, were the primary means of disposal. One end of each tube was tied shut by a slipknot with a long string and then, filled with dirt, the tubes were slipped inside a kriegie's trousers. The other end of each tube, along with the end of the string, was secured by the wearer's belt. The dirt was carried away by this method and sometimes hidden in a crawl space above a barracks ceiling or dumped into the latrine. Most of the soil, however, was hidden in plain sight, either on the grounds, or more often, in the garden which POWs were allowed to cultivate. The kriegie spreading dirt on the grounds would slowly shuffle around the compound, furtively releasing dirt and trying to smooth it out at the same time. He would be followed by two decoys also shuffling along and pointing to some nonexistent phenomenon in the sky to distract an alert guard from noticing their feet. Their slow, shuffling gait earned them an appropriate nickname. They were dubbed penguins. The garden was the easiest place to spread and mingle soil. It was simply spaded in around the vegetables growing there.

From the job of filling the tubes, I was promoted to penguin. It was really very awkward to pull the strings, dispense the dirt and move in a way that would not draw attention. One day, just as I returned to the barracks after a penguin stint, before I had time to clean off the sand, a team of German guards burst into the room for an unannounced search. I tried to slip into the background, but my suspicious behavior got their immediate attention. They marched me off to solitary. I guess a dirty kriegie was not too unusual, for I was not questioned and spent only one night in the cooler.

I made myself useful to the escape planners in other ways, also. I became an "Artful Dodger," hanging around wherever a supervised Russian might be making some repair and when he, accidentally on purpose, dropped a nail or a small piece of wire I would slyly let my cap fall over it. When I picked up my cap, I had a small but very useful piece of contraband. One day, as I was wandering aimlessly around the grounds, I noticed a Russian laborer who was repairing the warning wire staring intently at me. When he caught my eye he then stared fixedly at the ground. My heart gave an excited flutter, "What could it be?" When he left the area I strolled over as close to the wire as I dared and spotted a small mound of dirt. Using the "cap falling off the head" ruse once again, I found myself in possession of a real treasure, a crudely made but quite effective pair of wire cutters! I replaced the tool with a pack of cigarettes which I dropped on the ground, casually kicking some dirt over it, and stayed around until I saw the same man return and collect his reward. It was a fine trade. I was elated to be able to turn in to the escape group such a valuable tool.

I learned to make kriegie lamps which were used to provide light in the digging operations. Making these lamps required some skill if they were to burn correctly. The basics were easy, a klim can and the only totally inedible foodstuff included in the Red Cross parcels, the universally shunned margarine. The tricky part was fashioning the wick. Probably the best material for that purpose was a kriegie belt. By now my own waistline was reduced so much that I had several inches of belt to spare. A fine wire twisted around a piece of the ribbed fabric produced a good enough wick, but if the wick was not inserted into the margarine just right, it would burn up too quickly to be of much use. It took me several attempts before I got the knack of it.

Chapter 22

TUNNELER

"Be careful what you wish for; you just might get it!" I finally did get what I wished for, an invitation to become a tunneler and an escape list number. I was given number 42 and my buddy, Brandy, number 43. We were to go as a team and spent hours refining the plan we meant to put into effect once we were clear of the camp. We were going to make our way to a nearby airfield, skirt the land mines and steal a small single wing, one-seat observation plane. I would climb up onto the wing, crank the engine, then slip into the cockpit and tuck the crank under the seat. Brandy would clamber in over me and we'd take off for Sweden, only fifty or sixty miles away. Not the most practical of plans, perhaps, but good enough to keep our minds occupied and our spirits hopeful.

The barracks hiding the tunnel I was to work on had the usual coke burning stove which stood on a square of bricks cemented together. Four men could lift the brick base and stove aside, revealing the wood floor beneath. Cut through the floor was a hole about two feet square giving access to the tunnel. When the cut section of floor was replaced, we carefully smudged the edges with spills and dirt before putting back the stove with its brick base. The opening into the earth was covered by a woven mat with dirt spread over it, simulating the ground around. Leading down to the staging area about six feet below was, amazingly, a fence post! Bribery could evidently buy almost anything. Crude rungs made from pieces of metal were affixed to the post.

Now that my turn to dig had come, I began to have serious second thoughts. I stripped off my bulky clothing, donned a flight suit and a knitted cap that I could draw down over my face to keep from inhaling too much dust and pulled on a pair of gloves. With great trepidation and a strong sense of dread, I descended. I found myself in a room some four by six feet, stocked with bags for hauling the soil to the surface, boxes for the tunnelers to fill as they dug, buckets, scoops made from klim cans, mallets, rope and kriegie lamps. When I looked into the mouth of the tunnel I realized that the last thing I wanted to do was to crawl into that dark, ominous hole. I put on my poker face, not wishing to reveal the inner turmoil I felt, but the other two workers there that day seemed to be aware of my unease. They assured me that I would get used to the close quarters after a time or two. My pride would not let me back down, so lying on my stomach, I began to inch forward dragging myself along with my elbows and pulling the rope with the dirt box attached. The darkness was relieved only by the light of the kriegie lamps and the eerie shadows added to my strong sense of foreboding. About every fifteen feet I came upon a larger space, about three feet square, for emergency turnarounds. After a distance of some thirty feet, I found a large coil of rope which could be moved forward as the tunnel lengthened. Then, suddenly, I was up against the end wall. My heart was thundering in my ears and my breathing accelerated. I was experiencing a severe case of tunnel fright and I wanted out! I tried to slow down my breathing, screwed up my courage and started to scrape sand with my klim can scoop. I filled the dirt box as quickly as I could and gave the rope a tug, the signal for the helpers to drag the box back and empty it. After a few minutes the answering tug came and I pulled the rope, bringing the box sliding back up to me. It was quite cold in the tunnel, but I felt sweat dripping from my brow as I worked to fill the box again. I sent it on and this time I followed it, worming my way backward. I was quite relieved when I was finally out, but I did my best not to reveal just how much anxiety I truly felt.

Chapter 23

CAVE-IN!

In the days that followed, I tried to put fear of the tunnel out of my mind, but I couldn't forget how churned up my emotions had been and I was very apprehensive about returning. I knew that I could not let myself chicken out, though, and a couple of days later I went back to digging duty. For me it did not get any easier. I didn't dig every day, but every time I did go in, I just wanted to fill the dirt box as fast as possible and get out.

On my fourth turn I was about forty feet into that dark confining space, scraping away, with the dirt box almost full, when it happened. I heard a loud "whump!" and felt a crushing weight of sand suddenly pinning me to the tunnel floor and burying me up to my chest! My mind could scarcely accept the magnitude of the disaster! My worst nightmare had become reality! I was buried alive! I could feel the thudding of my heart in my throat but I told myself I must not panic. Dire thoughts began to race through my head. How far back did the cave-in extend? Would anyone even be aware of what had happened? Could they reach me in time? How long would the air in the small pocket around my shoulders and head last? I was afraid to shout for fear that more sand would be dislodged and I knew that no one could hear me. If only I had paid more heed to my premonitions and not brushed aside my misgivings! My predicament was more horrifying to me than even those last minutes in our ruined B-17 before I bailed out. There was nothing I could do here. I was totally helpless and I feared that my time had come. In the thick of battle many of my friends and comrades were killed and I knew my own death was very possible. I had accepted that, but I didn't want to die like this—in icy cold suffocating darkness.

After an eternity in that silent, black tomb, I felt something touch one of my feet! My heart leaped, but I was careful to lie absolutely still, afraid that the sand above my head would collapse and smother me. Hands clasped my ankles and with tugs and yanks my body was slowly being hauled backward. I tried to hold my breath, but reflex took over and I inhaled, choking on the dirt. With a final "whoosh" I was clear of the cave-in. Backing up on his belly, my rescuer dragged me out of the tunnel. When we reached the staging area I was in a fog and I do not remember any words that were spoken. I only know my digging clothes were stripped off and I was helped into my own clothing. Someone walked me back to my barracks where, still dazed, I crawled into my bunk and curled up in my blanket, a much subdued warrior. I had just had the hell scared out of me and I felt totally isolated, like someone washed up on a desert island. I didn't want to talk to anyone and I wanted no one to commiserate with me. My roommates respected what I was going through and left me alone.

I remained curled up about a day and a half, pondering the meaning of it all. Finally, hunger won out over the intense horror I continued to feel as I relived in my mind my very narrow escape. My stacked up rations beckoned me and I re-entered the land of the living. I was soon fomenting new plans to plague my captors, but I never again went underground! I was sure the cave-in would rank as my worst wartime experience, but the future was to prove me wrong.

Chapter 24

ROCKET LAUNCHER

From where I was quartered, I could hear German voices and sounds of activity one or two fences away. Suddenly I had what seemed to me at the time a brilliant idea. I saw a way to harass the enemy! Unfortunately, it did not dawn on me that even such a small independent activity would need to be cleared by the oversight committee and I went ahead on my own. I scoured the camp for just the right weapons I was seeking, flat, smooth stones. With a couple that I judged to be just right in my pocket, I stationed myself by the concrete base of what had once been a watchtower, made sure I was screened from sight, reared back, spun around and heaved a rock over the fence, aimed, I hoped, so that it would rocket down on a German skull. I got away from the area as fast as I could, feeling really pumped by what I had done. A few days later I found a better spot for aiming, on the fence side of barracks 1. I let fly another missile and quickly slipped around the barracks and into a group of kriegies out for an afternoon walk.

After my third assault, as I was strolling around the grounds, I was suddenly bracketed by two German guards who turned me around and took me out of the compound. I hoped I was being picked up for some small infraction, such as being in the wrong area, but I was marched into headquarters and thoroughly searched. The search turned up two stones in my trousers pocket. The guards then examined my hands which were calloused, with broken and stained fingernails, fairly clear evidence that I had been engaged in activities which were rougher than reading and writing letters. I was sent to solitary. I was there for only three days, but they were days of worry and apprehension as to what might be in store for me. I was still unsure of the reason for my arrest.

From solitary I was taken to barracks 1, an American barracks, where I had been reassigned. I was commanded to appear before the barracks senior officer. Frankly, when I entered his room

I was amazed. It was a corner room measuring about sixteen by eighteen feet and contained beds for just four officers. The room was furnished with a table, some chairs, framed pictures on the walls, built in shelves containing boxes with Red Cross labels, and a fully functioning stove. It was warm and clean. The barracks chief was seated at the table which served as his desk and was obviously not pleased to see me. He ordered me to stand at attention and gave me the dressing down of my life. He told me I was a troublemaker, that I was causing dissension in the ranks, that my independent, unapproved rock throwing had jeopardized fellow prisoners and that hereafter I was to do nothing to cause repercussions of any kind. In my mind I was being told not to rock the boat. That did not sit well with me. My emotions got the better of me and I blurted out, "Sure, you would say that! Look at the way you live!" After a pregnant silence the captain ordered me out and told me he never wanted to hear of me again.

Chapter 25

BARRACKS LIFE

Barracks 1 was obviously a much better built structure than my previous assignment. It was cleaner and not nearly as cold. There was a brick firewall across the center which retained heat not only from the sun but also from the two hundred plus bodies housed there. This barracks had a faucet with running water and even a real flush toilet! The officers living there were tightly organized from top to bottom, the bottom being a "combine." I was assigned to a combine of plus or minus eight men including from time to time, Anthony (Tony) Abad, Norman Bodet, William Engel, David Ferris, Clyde (Mo) Freeman, Dudley Haddock, Dave Heibert, Orrin (Porker) Heinrich, Harold (Snookie) Mulford, Francis Shaw, George

Thom, and Thomas (Bobo) Underwood. We were responsible for keeping our immediate area clean and helping out as we could. If there was an elite prison housing assignment, this was it, but I was miserable. Among the two hundred prisoners in this barracks I knew no one, although over time some of these men became my very good friends. Most of my fellow inmates seemed to me to be "long timers" and appeared to have lost their spirit. Many were weak or ill and just stayed in their bunks all day. I found myself morosely contemplating the "if onlys." If only I hadn't grazed that Coke truck, I might be a fighter pilot today. If only I hadn't stayed at the Red Cross when I was on medical leave, the MP's would not have found me and I might still be flying missions. After I had run through the "if onlys" I thought about my parents. Did they know I was not dead, that I was a POW? How were they taking it? Whenever I found myself slipping into thoughts like these, however, and becoming melancholy, all I had to do was look around to realize I was comparatively well off. I saw guys who had lost arms or legs, had been badly burned, were missing parts of faces or had sustained other ghastly injuries. At least I was all in one piece and relatively healthy.

I began spending more and more time with my friends, the Brits and Americans in barracks 10 and 11. I enjoyed watching the soccer games between the Brits and the Yanks. Soccer was mostly a British sport in those days. The Americans were enthusiastic but clumsy, sometimes getting their feet completely tangled up with the ball, to the amusement of their opponents. After an errant kick, the Brits would shout, "Keep it on the island, mate! Keep it on the island!" One day a Yank came over to my barracks looking for me. They needed a fill in; would I play? It must seem a small thing, but I was elated. My spirits got a real boost. I wasn't very skillful, but I was speedy and I could kick a country mile. After that I played whenever I could. It was great to feel welcome somewhere.

As I became more familiar with the camp I learned what facilities and activities were available. There was a wash house in our compound, and now that the weather was warming up, we could bear to remove some of our clothing and subject it to a much needed scrubbing. The wash house was always crowded, though, and I saw that kriegies had devised a way to do laundry in their barracks. All that was needed was a bucket, a stick, preferably a piece of broom handle, and two pierced tin cans one fitting inside the other attached to the handle. They called this contraption a dobie. With a few frugal shavings from a bar of soap in the water and the dobie operating as a plunger we had our own crude washing machine. The fresh scent of a clean shirt was nothing less than glorious!

I continued to support escape attempts as much as I could. When an appeal was circulated for bed slats to be used for tunnel shoring, I willingly donated two. With only three slats remaining, my bunk was pretty uncomfortable, but I had observed how kriegie ingenuity could improve a bed and I followed the examples I saw. Barbed wire was everywhere in camp; there was a fence around the garden, one around the kitchen and one around the theater. You name it—there was a fence around it! Whenever we could gather a casual, innocuous appearing group close to barbed wire we could make it disappear rather quickly. Bending a strand back and forth would eventually cause metal fatigue, and with the help of a couple of buddies, I got enough wire to fashion a support for my burlap bag mattress. The tedious part was boring through the side boards. I took a small piece of wire and when our stove was in use, I heated it, hurried back to my bunk and charred and bored until a hole broke through. When I had enough holes made, I attached the wire, careful not to break the weakened board, and threaded it through in five places until I had used it all and had a flexible foundation supplementing my three slats. Surprise random searches by the guards repeatedly revealed our precious stolen wire which was always clipped and removed, rendering our hard work useless. I had to remake my bunk at least three times, but one thing the camp never ran out of was barbed wire! We were always on the lookout for anything that might improve our comfort. For example, whenever I noticed a shipping carton, if I thought I could get away with it, I would rip off a flap, hide it under my jacket, and slip it into my mattress under the shavings for a little extra support. Over time I constructed a relatively comfortable bed.

    I discovered that it was possible to check out shaving implements and I took advantage of that, even though they had to be returned immediately after use. Bathing was another matter. I was scheduled for a shower only three times in all the months I was incarcerated, but I got around that by being in the right place and fast on my feet. If someone was missing from the daily shower detail I was quick to volunteer to take his place. Thus, on any given day I might be Smith, Jones, or whoever, when the shower roll call was taken.

It seemed to me that a lot of the guys played cribbage, but cribbage didn't appeal to me. There was a camp library, and a number of my barracks mates read for hours at a time, lying in their bunks, but books were scarce and in much demand. I read *Tess of the d'Urbervilles* from cover to cover three times and would have read it yet again, but it was usually checked out. Actually I preferred to get outside every day as soon as possible to look for some kind of physical activity.

One day I noticed one of my roommates, Dudley Haddock, with a chess board. It was obviously homemade with a motley collection of chessmen. I had learned the rudiments of the game back in my cadet days, and when Dudley saw me looking at the board with interest he invited me to play. Thus began a real friendship where we whiled away many hours on that fascinating game. Dudley suffered, as did my friend, Brandy, from severe sinus infections and would also sometimes seek relief by pounding his head against the barracks wall. When he couldn't sleep, I would often stay up with him all night, just talking. Sometimes we would amuse ourselves listening to the "music" of what we called the *Snoring Symphony*, and compare the sounds and rhythms of the different instruments! In fact, that is how Porker got his nickname. He certainly wasn't fat. No kriegie was anything but quite lean, but his nighttime snorts did simulate certain barnyard noises!

After I had been in camp about a month, Mike Keesee, our co-pilot, turned up. I was certainly glad to see that he had survived. When he was captured his injuries were severe enough to require hospitalization for an extended period of time, and the leg that had been broken now appeared to be somewhat shorter than the other. Walking required a forearm crutch, but at least he was alive. Like so many of us he was reluctant to talk about what he had gone through.

The monotony of prison life was numbing to the spirit and any diversion was welcome. When one of my buddies called out the nickname they had given me, "Ferdie, Ferdie, come here! You've gotta see this!" I scrambled out the door to discover what he was so excited about and was astonished to see a squad of British POWs in their slightly shabby but full dress and neatly pressed uniforms marching briskly and jauntily and in perfect step around the parade grounds. They held their heads high and certainly did not look like ground down prisoners even though I knew that some of them had been captives three and even four years. I was impressed by their esprit de corps!

Another time I heard some rousing music which immediately transported me back to my days of football glory. It sounded like a marching band! I hurried to get as close as I could to see what was going on. What I saw certainly set me back on my heels! It was a small German military band which had paraded into the South compound to commemorate the discovery of one more exercise in futility—tunnel number fifty! Such lighthearted ragging of the prisoners, however, was soon to cease entirely and a much more punitive regime would set in.

Chapter 26

NEWS FROM A SECRET RADIO

Many of the prisoners were amazingly talented and quite inventive. While they could design and create costumes for the variety shows they staged, they could also copy clothing, both German military and civilian, for escape purposes. They could forge IDs, travel papers, passes, etc., that only the closest scrutiny might reveal as fake. Their most remarkable feat in my estimation was the construction, from contraband parts obtained through bribery, of a fully functioning radio. I later learned that there were actually two radios, each cleverly hidden, one in a barracks wall, the other in the theater, both in the West compound. The Germans deduced that the prisoners had a radio in their hands from the fact that we seemed very well informed regarding the progress of the war. Although diligent searches were conducted, the radios were never found.

Just as ingenious were the methods used to smuggle the news to other compounds and to each barracks. Some of the ruses used to disseminate the news bulletin included the use of a wristwatch with the works removed, copies wrapped around stones thrown from one compound to the other compounds, and a klim can with a false bottom. The camp mail courier brought this report, called the *POW-WOW*, into our compound hidden in his mouth! When the news was delivered to our barracks, we stationed a man at the front door and one at the back. If a guard was seen approaching our area, the warning, "Enemy up!" was given and everyone quickly assumed ordinary poses. Before my arrival, the more definitive, "Goon up!" was used, but the Germans finally learned the real meaning of "goon" and issued a command that disrespectful terms were not to be used in referring to the guards. If the coast was clear, the one who brought the news repeated it verbally to a small group gathered around him. The listeners would then go down the line to each room and again repeat the news to small groups.

We were allowed a newspaper by the Germans, *The Barth Hard Times*, but it contained only propaganda as far as war news was concerned. The paper was compiled, printed and disseminated but we took the information with a large grain of salt.

On June 6, 1944, the *POW-WOW* brought electrifying intelligence! D-Day, the invasion, was underway! We actually had this news before our captors did. The guards must have wondered at the manic behavior infecting the entire camp. Perhaps they thought manna had fallen from heaven because, surely, only a secret source of food could cause such excitement. Kriegies were cheering, bounding around, laughing, giving the existing version of high fives and shouting, "Home by Christmas!" The guards quickly took steps to quell the uproar and implemented their usual procedure calculated to dampen our spirits. Whenever kriegies became too boisterous, the guards would close intra-compound fences, effectively isolating us into smaller groups and cutting us off from friends. I, too, was exhilarated at first with the D-Day news, but the elation faded as I sat on my bunk and contemplated the long, arduous, uphill and bloody battles that must yet lie ahead.

Chapter 27

MENDING A BROKEN LEG THE GERMAN WAY

Prisoners were now pouring into the camp every day in large numbers, and new barracks in the North compound were being constructed to house them. In addition, the new prisoners who were injured meant that others had to be released from the hospital prematurely. These were assigned to a regular barracks even if they required considerable assistance from roommates. One such was assigned to our combine. When I met David Heibert, my heart went out to him. He not only had a cast on one arm, but also a leg cast that went from groin to ankle. He could neither sit nor stand, and personal hygiene required help from others. If all this were not misery enough, the German doctors had inserted maggots to eat away the dead flesh beneath his leg cast, and their greedy feeding kept Dave in agony day and night. In addition to his physical torment, there was the sickening odor of decaying meat which permeated our close quarters. Nights were the worst for him and in his suffering he would cry out and beg "somebody" to get the cast off. I'm sorry to admit that there was some mean-spirited grumbling about why he had to be in our barracks, but most of us just tried to help him get through his ordeal. He was another one I often sat up with and talked through the nights. A good night's rest would have been wonderful, but I couldn't sleep, anyway. I was always just too cold and too hungry. The day finally came when Dave's cast was removed. His bone had mended, but his convalescence was torture. The dead tissue on his leg had to be scraped off and a dressing applied, an extremely painful process that was repeated a number of times before he eventually returned to normal.

Chapter 28

ACTIVITIES

The camp provided various religious services, and I became an enthusiastic beneficiary of all blessings bestowed by the clergy. If the service was Anglican, I would attend. If the services were Protestant or Catholic I would attend those as well. For me, all the sermons were spiritually uplifting, and it was good to hear that we were not forgotten and that our cause was just.

I was out of my barracks every day, as long as possible, looking for some activity, anything, to relieve the monotony and the gloom inside. I found a promising area to hang around, just outside my barracks, as near the gate as I could get, because the various details that left from there often lacked a full complement and would take on a volunteer. I volunteered at every opportunity.

Shore detail was great because we were actually permitted to leave the camp. We all had to agree to parole, an ironclad promise not to try to escape while we were out. No one ever violated parole because we knew that if we did, the life of the detail leader would be forfeit. To be outside, to see trees and leaves up close, to watch the waves gently lapping the shore, to remove our boots and dip our toes into the surf, to smell the fresh sea air, I don't mean to wax poetic, but it was truly sublime! Rumor had it that some prisoners had actually been allowed to swim in the Baltic, but that never happened for us. We weren't out there to admire the scenery, though, we had work to do. We were cleaning up the shore for the Germans, true, but at the same time we might come upon marvelous finds to bring back to camp. What looked like scrap could find dozens of uses in talented hands. We were especially on the lookout for jetsam from crippled Allied planes trying to make it to neutral Sweden. I never saw any, but I did hear tell of it. Mostly we would find pieces of driftwood. If nothing else, clean white beach sand had many applications such as cleaning table tops, cleaning cooking pots and even cleaning teeth! One day I came upon two huge pieces of driftwood which I began dragging back toward the camp. I was surprised to find that I was not as strong as I thought I was, or used to be, and struggling to carry both pieces I began to lag behind the group. The German guard started angrily shouting, no doubt berating me, but I was dogged in my determination. Finally I realized the guard was getting really hot, and when his hand went toward his pistol, I ruefully gave up one of my prizes. I mourned that piece of wood for days!

Chapter 29

MORALE BOOSTER

The war was coming nearer now, and we could actually see flights of Allied bombers high above with their fighter escorts as they headed toward their targets. At first we were quite apprehensive concerning our own safety as the camp abutted a German flak school, clearly a violation of the Geneva Convention which prohibited military targets from impinging upon prison camps. An errant bomb aimed at the school could take out hundreds of prisoners. Soon, however, when we realized the Allies would never jeopardize us, an air raid siren would bring us out into the yard to wave our shirts, cavort around and cheer like excited sports fans! As German resistance crumbled and bombing targets were ever closer, the thundering noise and shock waves became tremendous! Strafing runs brought P-51's and P-47's with their aerial acrobatics close enough for us to feel we were almost part of the action. I'll never forget the P-51 that flew right over the camp, saluting us with a barrel roll! Our exultant spirits soon brought their punitive consequences. Orders came down from the German High Command requiring prisoners to remain in their barracks during air raids.

Chapter 30
NAZIS TIGHTEN CONTROL

After the abortive assassination attempt on Hitler's life in July, Stalag Luft 1 was removed from the jurisdiction of the Luftwaffe to the sterner and more punitive control of the Wehrmacht (army). Some pressure was brought to require Allied camp commanders to return a German officer's stiff arm, "*Heil, Hitler!*" salute in like manner, but that was never going to happen and a military salute in return was grudgingly allowed.

Anyone disregarding the edict to remain indoors during air raids could now be shot without warning. There was to be no leeway regarding disobedience. At least three prisoners that I heard of were killed, not being aware of the sirens or not getting indoors fast enough.

A new and ominous bulletin was soon posted in each barracks:

To All Prisoners of War!
The escape from prison camps is
no longer a sport!

There followed a long text spelling out the serious consequences of any future escape attempts.

Not long after this decree, as I was on one of my aimless walks around camp, I saw a great commotion seemingly centered on the end of my own barracks. A roll call was signaled and some two hundred occupants lined up for a head count. There was obviously a thorough search taking place, and I was thankful that I had on my person, as I did at all times, all my belongings, which, in addition to my priceless scarf, were just cigarettes and chocolate bars. Word came down the line that the ceiling in the end room had collapsed from the weight of tunnel sand which had been hidden there! Clothing was strewn around, mattresses flung outside on the ground, food packages torn open, etc., etc. Every inch of the room was searched as we all continued to stand in roll call formation. Hours passed but we were not allowed to break ranks to rest or for any other purpose. No tunnel was discovered and eventually, exhausted, we were permitted to re-enter our rooms. I could just imagine the frustration and anger of the guys who lived in that room with dirt everywhere and their few meager possessions ruined.

Chapter 31

THE RED CROSS AND THE YMCA

The International Red Cross and the YMCA did much to make life more bearable for the prisoners. They provided sports equipment such as baseballs and bats, soccer balls and nets, hockey sticks and ice skates. The hockey gear and ice skates were recalled, however, because kriegies found many contraband uses for the sticks and blades.

Sam Fogel, one of the three officers quartered with our barracks chief, had been a participant in the infamous 1936 Olympic Games held in Berlin where Hitler had spared no expense in providing a spectacular venue to celebrate Aryan superiority. An Olympic type high bar had been erected just outside our barracks and Sam, who was in excellent shape, often demonstrated his prowess with flips and strength maneuvers on that apparatus. His skill was amazing and watching him perform was a good show.

Some record players and records were also provided by these organizations. It was difficult to get hold of a phonograph, but one time we were lucky. We managed to check out a small suitcase sized record player, the kind that had to be cranked up to play, and a great record, *Don't Fence Me In*. We cranked and played that song nonstop day and night for as long as we were allowed to have it. Prisoners never entered any room other than their own without an invitation, but whenever a record was played in the vicinity, everybody would hang around outside and listen in. That night we attracted an enthusiastic crowd of sing along listeners in the hall. Fortunately there were several needles in the case, as we probably wore that one completely out!

Chapter 32
KRIEGIE HUMOR

A favorite pastime was trying to find some innocent way to annoy the guards. For example, we noticed that they often used the phrase, *"Was ist los?"* (What's wrong?) We mocked them by bastardizing the phrase. Using words that sounded German, but when translated were just nonsense, we would excitedly exclaim, "Die hunds ist loose! Die hunds ist loose!"

When we heard the guards, with puzzled expressions, saying bemusedly to one another, *"Was ist dis? Die Hund ist los! Die Hund ist los!"* (What is this? The dog is loose! The dog is loose!) we thought they looked comical and that gave us a laugh. Kriegies were hard up for any amusement!

Chapter 33

A LONG COLD WINTER

Now the days were growing shorter and the cold north winds beginning to blow. Soon we would find ourselves locked inside our barracks by 4:30 p.m. facing long, boring, frigid nights with little to occupy our minds. Some of the guys would lie in their bunks and read over and over letters they had received from home. It was hard to keep from sliding into depression as I watched them smiling to themselves. I never received any mail, not a single letter or package in all the months I was a prisoner. I wrote to my parents as often as camp regulations allowed, and I knew they must be writing to me but somehow my mail was going astray. I learned when I returned home after the war that they had indeed written to me and had sent me at every opportunity a box of the very finest Tampa cigars. No doubt some German officer enjoyed my cigars and destroyed the evidence of my folks' letters!

Carmen Miranda, the Brazilian Bomb Shell, she of the outrageous fruit filled chapeaux and ruffled, revealing rhumba gowns made an appearance in the South compound! Not in person, of course, but her impersonator was a dead ringer. The Broadway shows and musicals staged by the prisoners were marvels. All scenery and costumes were made from scraps, and all the roles, male and female, were portrayed by the men. Happily, I had an actual ticket for this show. There were always more wishful attendees than it was possible to accommodate even with multiple performances. When I entered to take a seat, I was astonished and I must admit more than a little resentful to see that the entire front row of seats was filled with German uniforms. I remember one chorus line where the dancers were endowed with large, bouncy falsies. As they bounced them up and down to a refrain of, "Oom-pah-pah! Oom-pah-pah!" the German officers guffawed appreciatively. As much as I enjoyed the show, I found Carmen Miranda's fruit filled hat more riveting than her bare midriff! Even if we couldn't get in to see a performance, it lifted the pervasive gloom if we could just hang around outside and hear sounds of delight, especially laughter!

I tried my hand at cooking for our combine and developed a specialty that my buddies praised highly. Since I didn't smoke cigarettes, I was sometimes able to trade for a few extras, such as powdered milk and maybe a little sugar. With a few contributions from my group, crushed crackers, some English marmalade, some raisins, even a shredded carrot and, worth its weight in gold, a little baking powder, I had the ingredients for a real treat. After I mixed all that with water and put the blob of batter into a homemade baking tin, I had to find the means to bake it. We couldn't spare precious coke for such a frivolous undertaking, but I could usually locate a room where the oven was going and I would be allowed space for my creation. "Ferdie!" one of the guys raved, as he slowly savored each morsel, making it last as long as possible. "You make a cake to die for!" Food! It was always uppermost in our minds.

November saw flocks of geese flying overhead on their migrations south, beautiful in their V-formation flights, symbols of freedom! Occasionally weather conditions would break up the formations and once a sleek, fat bird flew so low over the compound that I felt I could almost reach up and snag him. That "symbol of freedom" became in my mind crisply browned on a platter, bursting with my mother's savory bread dressing. In our house, the Thanksgiving bird was usually a somewhat older rooster who had, once too often, attacked my mother's ankles with his spurs, a little chewy maybe, but still quite satisfying!

In Stalag Luft 1 the canned Spam which came in the Red Cross parcels was everybody's favorite food item. Consequently, dividing the contents of a can with rounded ends was a serious undertaking. One tin had to serve eight men, each one watching, hawk-eyed, to determine if the portions were precisely equal. Everyone involved had advice and recommendations, but we solved the dilemma by having the cutter be the last to get his share. In our combine we had each been saving a little from our scanty rations so that we could enjoy a Thanksgiving feast. We held a long confab deciding whether to keep our can of tasty Spam or trade it for two cans of tasteless English corned beef. We reasoned that the corned beef, if mixed with potatoes, would be much more filling. We opted for the trade.

Thanksgiving, for the Americans, was a day filled with memories. I attended the morning church service and also the afternoon service. I spent the rest of the day reminiscing about my home, my family, my friends and especially the dinner my mother would have lovingly prepared which in retrospect was nothing less than a banquet! I remembered how I had casually and thoughtlessly eaten whatever I wanted, whenever I wanted it. By now I had developed a respect, bordering on reverence, for even a slice of sawdust bread! That evening we relished our frugal feast.

The first winter snowfall brought many of us out of our barracks to watch the pristine flakes drift down. Snow covered the ugliness of the camp and softened the harsh reality that lay beneath. Snow was beautiful—for maybe a day. After that it became a nuisance, and finally a hindrance. As winter progressed, the snow became deeper and deeper until one morning when Porker and I started out to fetch ersatz coffee for the twenty some men in our room we found the snow was up past our knees. Each carrying two large, metal pitchers, we took turns ramming through the drifts. I would ram a couple of yards, step back and he would ram.

When we finally reached the coffee dispensing site there was no one there! The German guards were in no hurry to report in such miserable cold. We waited around stamping our feet and shivering until they showed up. Carrying the heavy full pitchers, at least we had a cleared path back to our barracks.

Chapter 34

THE UNINVITED!

After lights out our room was in total darkness except for a little feeble illumination from the camp perimeter lights which filtered through the closed shutters. A group of us who found sleep elusive were sitting around just talking when suddenly, in the shadows, we noticed a stealthy movement! We had an uninvited night visitor! As one, we froze in position as we watched the intruder. He was as quiet as a mouse, since that was what he was, a little field mouse who had slipped in from the ground below through a hole no bigger than a grape. We watched in silent fascination as he crept about looking for some small scrap of food. He found a crumb on the floor, daintily picked it up and hurriedly ate. Some movement alerted him to our presence and he quickly scurried back through the hole. We were delighted and immediately made plans to bait the hole to see if our visitor would return. Sure enough, the following night that mouse, or maybe a different one, took the bait, devoured his little treat and left. Now our excitement turned to thoughts of capture. We would tame him and keep him as a pet. He certainly ate very little and could be a source of much amusement. The next night we gathered in a tight circle around the hole with our hands shielding our faces so our breathing would not alert him. As soon as he had cautiously entered, two of us pounced, one sliding something over the hole to prevent his escape and the other trying to get a box over the mouse without injuring him. The rest of us tried to keep him within the circle. There was only one problem with this plan. He was faster than any of us and our box always came up empty. Many a night we matched our skills to his in frantic attempts to catch him. We had lots of laughs but no success and finally left our house guest to his own pursuits.

Chapter 35

THE BATTLE OF THE BULGE

The sixteenth of December brought some disturbing war news. The Germans had launched a powerful counteroffensive on the European front which became known as the Battle of the Bulge. They threw everything they had into this final struggle to drive the Allied forces from Europe. Their efforts were initially quite successful as they seemed to be regaining ground daily. Gone were our hopes to be "Home by Christmas." Our faith was strong in an eventual win by our forces, but we had to resign ourselves to a dreary, seemingly interminable winter.

The seventeenth of December brought, along with the usual daily arrivals, an especially noteworthy prisoner. Colonel Hubert Zemke, an ace fighter pilot, joined our ranks. From the beginning we had maintained a military chain of command in the camp. When I arrived, Colonel Jean Byerly was the SAO, the Senior Allied Officer. Other American officers prominent in the command structure included Colonel Ross Greening, an accomplished artist, Colonel H. R. Spicer, whose feisty nature landed him the cooler more than once, Colonel E. A. Maelstrom, Lt. Colonel C. Wilson, and Lt. Colonel F. S. Gabreski. When Colonel Zemke arrived he found himself to be the SAO, and, ready or not, required to shoulder a multitude of problems and responsibilities. He proved himself more than equal to the task. Since the American top brass were all quartered in the North compound, I had no personal interaction with any of them but all prisoners were kept informed of important decisions and contingencies.

Chapter 36

CHRISTMAS NOSTALGIA

A sprinkling of Christmas decorations appeared here and there, mainly on the theater/library/chapel building. Religious symbols were avoided in favor of Santa, scantily festooned with crepe paper. A few lucky kriegies received packages from home, and one entrepreneurial type parlayed an unusual item he received into a windfall of cigarette dollars. Excitement, like a current of electricity, was running through the compound. "You can't miss this! If you've two cigarettes to spare you've got to go and get in line!" I joined a line that snaked completely around a barracks and out into the yard. With my two cigarettes in hand, I chafed at the slow moving queue until I was finally there. It was my turn! The proud owner of a possession creating so much commotion held his prize in both hands. It was a glass jar filled with amber liquid in which were floating a number of round, dark objects—brandied cherries! For my two cigarettes I was allowed two deep inhalations of this nectar. I held my second breath as long as I could as I made way for the next one in line. I gave up two more cigarettes the following day for another turn at such a luxury. Was the experience worth the fee? Absolutely!

I observed Christmas by attending church services and again I was present at every service where there was room enough to squeeze in. Other celebrations included Christmas music and choral singing provided by prisoner musicians and a Christmas dinner greatly enhanced by special extra Red Cross parcels. We all tried to remain upbeat and appreciate what we had, but I knew that many of my friends were thinking of wives and children they had not seen, perhaps for years, and brooding over the happy plans they had made for "Home by Christmas." Now that bubble had burst and faded away.

Chapter 37

AN UNEXPECTED ACQUAINTANCE WITH HOSPITAL STAFF

The harshest winter in fifty years was rolling over Europe. In our latitude the cold was intense, merciless and paralyzing. No one left the room without a compelling reason. In fact, we didn't leave our bunks if we didn't have to. I tried to keep my breathing shallow to avoid taking frigid air too deeply into my lungs. Whenever the door did open, I held my breath altogether against the even colder air that pushed in. I wrapped up in everything I owned and kept my boots on even during the night. I longed for the blessed nirvana of sleep but was so miserably cold that sleep was fitful if it came at all.

At any given time one or more of the guys in our room would be down with some malady. None of us ever wanted to add to anyone else's burdens and kept our troubles to ourselves, so when I began to feel ill and nauseated I didn't complain and hoped it would just pass away. It didn't! I continued to feel worse and worse as day became night. I began to sweat profusely and couldn't think of eating anything. My temperature soared and then the cramps began, followed by stabbing abdominal pains. I tried to make it through until morning, but about 2:00 a.m. I couldn't take it any longer and couldn't hold back groans of pain. Dudley became alarmed and roused the others in our combine. Someone was sent to the barracks headquarters room to inform the officers there of my predicament. The German guards were summoned and soon two orderlies from the South compound hospital barracks arrived. They put me on a stretcher, covered me with a blanket and began to carry me through the blowing snow to the hospital.

A guard passed us through one double gate, closing and locking it behind us. Suddenly, in the distance, through the haze of snow, another guard appeared. He shouted, *"Halt!"* and, not waiting for a response, released his dogs. The two guys carrying me, fearing for their lives, dropped me in the snow and ran. The dogs were on me in a moment, snarling and barking, so close that I could feel their hot breath as drops of their saliva hit my face. I fully expected them to tear into my flesh with their fangs, and—I just didn't care. For the first time I thought I might be better off dead. The dogs, however, although they continued to snuffle around the stretcher, did not attack me. I couldn't move, but I was aware of a lot of activity and then my stretcher was picked up again and I was delivered to the hospital barracks.

Dr. Nicholls, a British neurosurgeon, was there when I arrived. When he gently touched my abdomen my reaction convinced him that there could be no waiting. Immediate surgery, for acute appendicitis, was mandatory, and I was given a shot of something that, thankfully, eased the terrible pain.

The room I was in appeared to be some sort of mess area, empty except for some wooden tables. One of the tables was pulled to the center of the room, draped with a white sheet and some portable lights were positioned over it. When I was placed on the table and strapped down, I realized that this cold, bare room was the doctor's operating theater! I was aware of considerable hurried movement around me as his aides brought in and unpacked the supplies and instruments Dr. Nicholls would use. I heard the word "ether" a number of times and came to the realization that there was none available. Dr. Nicholls sent an aide to the German hospital area, but when he returned empty-handed I knew that the general anesthesia I was anxiously awaiting was not an option for me.

Dr. Nicholls' assistant was Lt. Smythe, a black RAF officer from Rhodesia, who had been a medical student before he joined the war effort as a navigator. Unfortunately I overheard Dr. Nicholls complaining bitterly to Smythe, "Look at these instruments! Just look at what I have to operate with!" words not calculated to ease anxiety! When he was ready to begin surgery, the doctor stationed two aides at my head who, upon his signal, injected a vein on either side of my neck. I did not lose consciousness, but no longer felt any pain.

I had always imagined, if I thought about it at all, that a surgeon, with his finely honed scalpel, would begin an incision with the grace and deftness of a violinist drawing his bow across the strings. Not so! Dr. Nicholls plunged his knife into my body with such force that I thought he would surely pierce me entirely and pin me to the table! Although I felt no pain, I felt the pressure and heard the sounds as he cut through muscle and tissue. The incision revealed the gravity of my condition—my appendix had ruptured, spewing bloody pus over other organs. Now the incision had to be extended so that Dr. Nicholls could flush out all the poisonous matter. This he did with what appeared to me to be an ordinary garden hose!

When the team was ready to close they discovered more bad news. There were not enough staples on hand to close such an extensive incision, and they had to improvise which they did by spacing the staples as far apart as they dared. Two of the men held the bunched together flesh while a third drove the staple through. By now whatever had been injected into my jugular veins had worn off and I felt the sharp pain of each and every puncture. When I finally did return to the States and was examined by an Army doctor, he jokingly asked me, "Where did you get that scar? Did you have a Cesarean?" I couldn't appreciate his humor!

The ordeal finally over, I was moved to another location and fell sound asleep. Frankly, I don't know if I slept for a day, two days, or even a week, but when I did wake up, my immediate perception was of warmth! Wherever I was it was warm, blissfully warm! I tried to turn my head but found that I was completely immobilized. My field of vision included only what I could see by cutting my eyes from left to right and down. I couldn't see much. An orderly seated at a raised desk, noticing that I was awake, came over, greeted me, offered some water and later, some soup. The days that followed are indistinct in my memory, but I know I was cared for solicitously by the staff. When I began to be more aware and interested in my surroundings, someone placed a concave mirror where I could see part of the ward. That thoughtful act greatly relieved the monotony. After what I judged to be several weeks, the flat board I was strapped to was raised to a slant so that I had a better view of the ward and could watch the goings on. My convalescence was slow, but eventually, after the wound had stopped weeping, the drain had been removed and the staples taken out, I was helped from bed to try a step or two. A step or two was all I could manage. The orderlies constructed a contraption which allowed me to be semi-erect on my board with my body supported by my arms, thus avoiding problems that constantly lying prone would produce. In this leaning position I could, and often did, fall asleep.

Dr. Nicholls became a hero in my mind. Not only did his skill and that of his staff under terribly adverse circumstances save my life, but he was tireless and inventive trying to improve conditions for his patients and raise morale. I learned that Dr. Nicholls had been captured during the disaster of Dunkirk and had been a prisoner for more than four years, but I never saw him dispirited or out of sorts.

The good doctor was fervent in his belief that hygiene was of paramount concern in prison camp, and following this precept, he earnestly recommended to incoming patients scheduled for surgery that, since they would be under anesthesia anyway, they should take advantage of the situation and permit circumcision. Proof of his success in this campaign came one day when, amid uproarious laughter, he entered the ward dressed in imitation of a Revolutionary soldier, playing a fife and smartly marching around the room, along with a drummer and a standard bearer. The standard bearer proudly carried a broom handle from which hung a very small banner. The banner, attached by a cord, was—someone's foreskin! I was witnessing my first "Foreskin Parade!"

As I regained my strength and mobility I tried to make myself useful. I could reposition a patient, bring a drink of water, wipe a perspiring brow, secure a slipping bandage, and probably most welcome, scratch an unreachable itch.

One day I heard some tapping that sounded like metal on metal coming from another room, and expecting to see patients playing some sort of game, I entered. What I saw was no game. An orderly using a chisel was trying to loosen flak imbedded through the meat of a leg and into the bone. Many POWs had shrapnel lodged in their bodies and endured their fate in silence, but the sub-zero temperatures of this winter could make the metal more agonizingly painful to bear than suffering the removal of it.

I thought for a time that I had found my niche as an aide in the hospital barracks but eventually the unending misery all around got to me. The hospital had a "no visiting" policy and I missed my friends. I greatly admired the dedicated men who devoted themselves to the welfare of their ill and wounded comrades, but I just wanted to go "home." I was still too weak to walk the distance from the hospital to my own barracks, so I was bundled onto a stretcher and delivered to my room.

An odor of musty boots, less than strictly clean clothing and cooking permeated the room. It smelled wonderful! I was warmly welcomed and found that my buddies had restuffed my mattress with fresh wood shavings, had made a precious piece of canvas into a pillow and had put a new blanket, neatly folded, on top of the old one. What a homecoming!

Chapter 38

CONDITIONS WORSEN

According to the calendar, winter was over, but frigid temperatures continued to plague us. By now it was obvious to everyone that the German counteroffensive had failed and that Germany had lost the war. Still the fighting continued and more prisoners arrived every day. There were no longer materials for constructing any additional barracks and the newcomers had to live in miserable conditions in tents.

Our food supply seemed to dwindle daily as Red Cross rations were cut and cut again. The German contribution became even sorrier than before. In our share of potatoes at least a few were always frozen and rotten. The occasional rutabaga, which I had so cavalierly spurned when I first arrived, was now a real prize. I saw men so weak from hunger that they could no longer stand upright. Everyone heard the story of the cat that unfortunately strayed into camp. The next morning, the cat was gone, replaced by a small pile of bones! I no longer even thought of escape, but concentrated my efforts on staying alive.

Ominous rumors were circulating, becoming stronger at each repeating. Escapees would no longer be returned to camp, but shot as spies. Jewish prisoners were to be segregated into separate barracks, for what villainous purpose we hardly dared to imagine. Markowitz sought me out and gave me a sealed envelope which he asked me to deliver to his parents in case he did not make it back to the States. I assured him that I would do so. I was greatly relieved when I was able to return it to him. A belief was taking hold that all of the nine thousand plus prisoners in Stalag Luft 1 would be moved to some other location and none would ever know freedom again.

By now, in early April, the cold had mitigated and the ground had thawed, but the food shortage was becoming critical and morale was eroding. We began to believe that we were methodically and intentionally being starved.

Chapter 39

LIBERATION!

Suddenly, overnight, everything changed! In the depths of famine, a veritable feast appeared! Red Cross food packages, which had been hung up somewhere, arrived by the truckload! Even potatoes from the Germans were more abundant! Adequate food was available now, but we knew that overeating could be dangerous. We still ate small portions, only a little more frequently. Easter services that week swelled with joyful men giving thanks.

The demeanor of our German guards also changed. Strict authoritative attitudes were clearly softening, our captors trying to demonstrate that they weren't such bad guys after all. Max Schmeling, the World Heavyweight Boxing Champion, visited our camp, apparently on some sort of goodwill tour. This event created considerable excitement, many POWs eager to see such a celebrity. I didn't bother to leave my room, unimpressed with this superficial show of camaraderie.

It was payback time for the Russians who had mounted a *Blitzkrieg* (lightening war) of their own and were rolling across northern Germany. Day and night the thunder of their artillery bombardment continued, growing closer and closer. Emotions were running high. Shouts of, "*Ruski*, come!" were heard over and over. We were elated at the thought of rescue, yet apprehensive about what sort of reception we would experience once we were in Russian hands. There was also a growing fear that we might become accidental targets of the shells. Word came down that slit trenches and fox holes were being dug, but that enterprise was undertaken essentially in the North compound where new arrivals still had the strength for digging. I saw none of that in the South or West compound.

Early on the morning of May 2, 1945, I was awakened by sounds of men shouting, laughing and cheering! I hurried out to see what was happening, but it was what I didn't see that was riveting! There were no German guards manning the towers! The gates between the compounds had been removed! There were no guards to be seen anywhere! Our captors had cleared out! Kriegies were kriegies no longer!

Jubilation quickly turned into pandemonium! Life in Stalag Luft 1 changed from strict regimentation to confusion bordering on chaos. Men were running in every direction—their destinations I couldn't guess. Some attacked the fences, tearing them down. I thought that a foolish waste of strength and energy, but the symbolism of fences was just too much for some to stomach any longer. Explosions and shots rang out from the direction of the flak school. I later learned that German civilians had attempted to storm the facility and loot the Red Cross food parcels stored there. They were routed but not before they had made off with a number of the boxes.

A group of us, relying on safety in numbers, decided to hike into Barth to see what sights we could. It was a longer walk than we had thought and in our weakened condition, very tiring. When we arrived, there was nothing to see. The Russians had decreed that all civilians must be off the streets by 8:00 a.m. Any necessary activities had to be completed between daybreak, at about 4:30 a.m., and that hour. Any time civilians were out, they were required to wear white, or have a white banner pinned to their clothing.

When I returned from the city, I heard that there was an emergency call for assistance from the hospital and I went over to see if I could lend a hand. Some of the guys had found their way into the German stores and helped themselves. They had filled their stomachs with barley with disastrous results. When I reached the hospital barracks, an overpowering stink enveloped me before I even set foot in the door. Inside there was bedlam around a grisly scene. I saw men lying unconscious on tables, their abdomens split open with their intestines heaped up beside them. The barley they had eaten had bloated, clogging their insides so severely that nothing could pass. The medical staff members were frantically massaging the intestines, trying to milk the waste matter on through. There was obviously nothing I could do to help and not wanting to be in the way, I left. I prayed that those poor wretches might make it.

Three of my friends, Dudley Haddock, Mike Keesee, Snookie Mulford and I discussed the pros and cons of striking out on our own, heading west to try to connect with British forces. We decided to walk through the woods to the seashore and consider our options. On that picturesque, sandy beach, the real horror of war finally overwhelmed me. Sprawled along the shore were corpses of murder and suicide victims, the flies already gathering. Men from the camp were hollowing out pits in the sand to bury the bodies and appealed to us for help. I took a shovel and began digging a grave for a family of four. Two beautiful little children, a girl and a boy, and their mother were dead from gunshot wounds. The father had then turned the pistol on himself and, in a last futile gesture of protection, had flung his body over theirs. Here was an ordinary working man, who very probably had never had a political thought in his life, just trying to rear his children, provide for his family and live his life, a man who had felt compelled to choose the death of his loved ones over the dread of what retribution from Russian conquerors would bring. I was so overwrought that I couldn't tell you who was standing next to me as we worked, but when we finished with that grave, I jammed the shovel into the sand, turned away and, with my three friends, left Stalag Luft 1 forever.

Russians arrive

Guard tower demolished

Chapter 40

AN ERROR IN JUDGMENT

As usual, we had all our worldly possessions on our persons, so we just walked on, wondering how we should proceed, when we spotted an old wooden boat shoved up under some brush and decided to row across the inlet to begin our westward trek. There was a plank in the boat and another piece of wood that could be used as oars. We noticed that there was also some water in the boat and tried to turn it over, but it was too heavy, so taking our chances, we climbed in and began rowing. After we passed the point of no return we realized that the water level in the bottom of the boat was slowly rising. We rowed furiously, but we didn't make it. About twenty yards from the bank the boat hit bottom. Thankfully, the water at this point was only about three feet deep and we were able to wade ashore. When I took stock of my food stash, I found that my one precious piece of bread was quite soggy. I ate it anyway. It was easier to chew and the salt water actually improved the taste!

In retrospect, leaving the safety of Stalag Luft 1 was an error in judgment. Although we reached the repatriation center in Paris a full week before the ex-POWs who remained at the camp, along the way we found ourselves witnesses to the inhumanly cruel and tragic consequences of war. The first night we were concerned only as to where we might sleep and if we would be able to find food. I really can't say where we were, but we came upon a building resembling a gymnasium where many German families consisting of women, children, and old men were taking shelter for the night. Young men were conspicuously absent. There was food available which they kindly shared with us. After we ate we bunked down on the floor for the night. Several of the families entrusted me with messages to deliver when we joined the British forces, hoping that I might be able to intervene for their sons and husbands who were prisoners in America.

If it had not been for Mike Keesee, I believe I would never have seen home again! Mike could speak Polish and was able to communicate with the Russians whose army we encountered the next day. Shouting, *"Amerikanski! Amerikanski!"* we gave ourselves into their custody. The Soviet officers seemed to be reasonable men. They gave us food and permission to accompany them as they marched, unopposed, toward the Elbe River. The troops, however, were something else, a fearsome company of wild, savage Cossacks drunkenly thundering around on their horses, brandishing sabers. They offered us vodka, and by crude hand signals, invited us to join them in their pursuit of the spoils of war, plunder and women. They were our liberators but I found them repulsive.

Hitching rides as we were able, or otherwise on foot, we made it to the Elbe River where everything came to a halt. The politics of war decreed that the Russians would stop on the eastern side of the river and the British on the western side at the city of Wismar. We thought we would be crossing over to the British forces immediately, but Russian protocol didn't allow that. The Soviet ranking officer was a colonel, but the British had only a major available and the colonel refused to negotiate with anyone of lesser rank. We spent the next several days in the Russian encampment.

Captured Germans had been stripped of anything military, entire uniforms as well as coats, gloves, caps, boots, etc., and stores of those items were available for the taking. I left my friends where they were and went foraging to see if I could find a better pair of boots for myself. Suddenly I was surrounded by Cossacks. My shouts of, *"Amerikanski! Amerikanski!"* fell on deaf ears. One of them threw a choke noose around my neck and I was roughly propelled toward a long line of captured Germans trudging eastward to lives as slave laborers in the USSR.

I heard Mike calling my name, "Ferdie! Ferdie! Where are you?"

I yelled back as loudly as I could, "Mike! Mike! Over here!" He came running up and speaking Polish was able to convince my captors to let me go free. After that I did not venture far from the officers' area.

A Soviet captain invited us to take a short trip with him so that he could show us why captured Germans were given no mercy. He took us to a German slave labor camp. What I saw stunned me! We've all seen, on television or in films, the horror of those camps, but to be there in person was enough to strain one's sanity! What seemed to be acres of emaciated corpses, eyes staring, mouths agape, had been bulldozed into a mountain of dead bodies. Of all the world's species, only man is capable of such evil!

At long last, the British produced a colonel. My own guess was that the major received a temporary spot promotion! The Russian colonel kissed each of us on either cheek and sent us on. What a relief! We went from Russian chaos to British order. The Brits couldn't do enough to spoil us. They treated us as the officers we were, with full courtesies. They provided us with hot food at any hour and comfortable sleeping quarters. They invited us to visit local merchants whose wine cellars were open to us along with stores of fine cheeses and other delicacies. The merchants were pleased to serve us because, although we could take anything we wanted, we signed for the items and the merchant would be reimbursed by the occupying forces. There was a vast difference in the treatment of the defeated on the eastern banks of the Elbe compared to the western. We were encouraged to help ourselves to the German memorabilia available. I chose Luger pistols, medals, daggers inscribed with *"Deutschland uber Alles,"* and various other items. Unfortunately, I did not make it home with these souvenirs as they were stolen from me upon my return to the States.

The officer who was chauffeuring us around as we happily sipped wine and munched on cheese took us to see something he said we would never forget. Some miles on through the ruined countryside he stopped at a part of the river where we learned that the British, also, had exacted retribution. The river was clogged with bodies of men in full dress black uniforms bearing the death's head insignia. They were the brutal, hated and feared German SS officers. Their captors had forced them to march into the river and had launched metal nets over them slowly drowning them all. Our blithe spirits came crashing down at this sobering revelation. In war, every man is capable of atrocities.

Chapter 41

PARIS!

A C-47 transport aircraft was loading up for a flight to Paris. In addition to those who had official business there, the passengers included all the ex-POWs who could squeeze on board. I sat on the floor in the aisle along with my friends. The trip was a short one and we soon found ourselves in Paris. The date was May 8, 1945, proclaimed as Victory in Europe—VE—Day! There was rejoicing everywhere, everyone in a holiday mood! My first destination in town was a debriefing center. My identity established, I was given an ID card on a cord to wear around my neck. I was required to strip and bathe. I thought that was the end of it, but no, a medic said, "Okay, sir, turn around and bend over." A sudden loud blast from a compressed air apparatus smoked me with delousing powder! After that I was provided with new GI issue clothing, trousers, shirt, jacket, boots, and my officer's insignia which I could pin on.

My next stop was a Red Cross canteen for something to eat. There was real coffee, hot soup and fresh hot bread without a trace of sawdust! The Red Cross ladies were going around passing out goodies, including Baby Ruth candy bars. What a treat they were! From there I went to a shelter barracks, took off my boots which I tied to my belt, and slept for about an hour. I was then delivered to Camp Lucky Strike, the repatriation center. One look at me—I've already said I exhibited considerable body hair—raised suspicions. The reception committee was taking no chances. I was deloused again!

The next morning after an enriched milk shake breakfast, I hopped on a mail truck and rode it back to Paris. I saw sights I never expected to see. I strolled along the Champs Élysées where, by the way, I was surprised to notice public urinals, at least one in every block! I walked through the Arc de Triomphe, saw the Eiffel Tower, shopped a bit and bought myself a smart beret. I ate at a Red Cross canteen but had no place to stay for the night. Someone there found me billeting in a private home where, for one night, I slept on a feather bed with a goose-down comforter!

Chapter 42

STOWAWAY!

The next day, at the canteen, eating my favorite breakfast of hot bread and butter topped with sugar, I very unexpectedly saw a friend from Glatton, George Cahelo, who had completed at least forty missions and was the most highly decorated bombardier in the Eighth. As we drank our coffee and talked, I shared with him my desire to get to England to see my brother who was still stationed at High Wycombe. George mulled that over and said, "I'll tell you what we'll do. We'll stow you away on the B-17 my crew is taking back to Glatton today!" We rode a truck to the airfield where George pointed out which plane was his and said they'd be leaving in an hour. As unobtrusively as I could, I slipped on board and concealed myself in the radio operator's compartment where the nacelle covers were usually stored. I tossed two of the covers out, got a blanket to cushion the vibration and covered myself with maps. We took off without my being discovered and I tried to get a little sleep. I was always tired. When the radio operator opened the cabinet, he was quite startled and demanded to know who I was. When he realized I was an ex-POW from the 457th, he became very solicitous and shared his food ration with me. When we landed I waited until the coast was clear and made for the Officers' Club bar. Everyone shook my hand, or clapped me on the shoulder, delighted to see me. When they realized I was in England without any money they immediately took up a collection—even the bartender contributing—and presented me with about thirty British pounds, some hundred twenty American dollars. I wandered around and found a room full of various parts of officers' uniforms, jackets, boots, etc., from guys who had not returned. Probably my own clothes were in there somewhere! The place looked like a church rummage sale, and I rummaged around until I had outfitted myself, even down to the dapper crushed cap. I then burrowed into the piles of clothes and fell asleep.

The next day I got a lift into Glatton, took the train to Peterborough, the tram to High Wycombe and found my brother, Ferdie. The first thing I remember was his comment, "You can't go home looking like that! We'll have to fatten you up a little!" He took me into London to the famous Dorchester where one could visit the American Bar, the English Bar, and the European Bar. We visited them all. I also remember staying at the Maidenhead Hotel in one of the very rooms used by the Duke and Duchess of Windsor. It was a beautiful place, with the resident swans still serenely swimming in the lake.

Chapter 43

GOING HOME

I had enjoyed only a few days with Ferdie when we received alarming news. Colonel Zemke, who was the Senior Allied Officer when Stalag Luft 1 was liberated, was adamant that any ex-POW who had left camp on his own should be court-martialed! Good sense decreed that I must return to Camp Lucky Strike ASAP, which I did. Since I finally had all required identification I was not deloused this time! I went by a small boat to Southampton to await a ship to the States. There was no ship immediately available, and not wanting to just hang around, I returned once more to London and spent a few more weeks with Ferdie. He finally convinced me that I really needed to go home, so it was back to Southampton one more time!

The Queen Elizabeth and the Queen Mary had both been pressed into service as troop carriers, but I naively requested the first ship available. Mistake! It was the SS Argentina, a former cargo ship, with a Brazilian crew. The troop bunks were sixteen high and the trip would take twice as long as the large ships. I worked a deal with one of the ship's officers. For five dollars a day he would let me sleep in his quarters while he was on duty and would slip me some of his rations.

One day out of our destination, Newport News, Virginia, a hurricane struck! The captain decided to ride it out, and for two days the ship pitched and rolled in the storm. Seasickness was widespread and the deck was slick with puke from one end to the other! I have never experienced sea sickness and for that I am truly thankful!

Chapter 44

THERE'S NO PLACE LIKE HOME

Immigration paperwork completed, I boarded a troop train to Camp Blanding and was soon on my way home. I reached Tampa about 10 p.m. and stayed overnight at the Floridian Hotel. The next morning, the Fourth of July, 1945, I caught a cab to my house in Ybor City and knocked on the door. My parents knew I was coming home, but didn't know just when I would arrive. When my mother answered the door, she shouted for my dad, "*José! José!*" He came running to the door and then I was smothered in their embraces. The three of us just stood there for a few moments, and I remember that my mother kept touching my face and my arms as if to make sure that I was not an apparition that might disappear.

Everything seemed just as I had left it. The air was thick with emotion that day, but my folks didn't have a lot to say. They mostly just sat and looked at me while we sipped the *café con leche* my mother had prepared. During the next several days, as I became reacquainted with my surroundings, I noticed that my parents seemed to watch my every move. Whenever I caught them gazing at me, they averted their eyes, not wanting to make me self-conscious, and my mother would brew yet another pot of *café con leche*.

After Victory in Japan—VJ Day—when we learned that my brother, Frank, was safe, I turned my thoughts to taking up my real life again. I still intended to go to the University of Florida, although football for a guy weighing scarcely a hundred pounds was out of the question. Before I enrolled, however, another of those twists of fate intervened and determined my future. The board members of Florida State College for Women, in Tallahassee, decided to admit three hundred returning veterans as students. When I received the letter asking if I would be interested in attending, I sent a return letter, a telegram and I telephoned saying, "Yes! Yes!" and, "Yes!"

At Florida State I met a young co-ed, of German heritage yet! After fifty-four years, four children and four grandchildren, we are still together, but that's another story.

These children were killed by their father who also killed their mother and himself rather than allow the family to fall into Russian hands.

Appendix

World War II aircraft referred to in the memoirs

PT-17 Stearman,
American Primary Trainer

P-47, American Fighter Escort

B-17G, American Bomber

P-51, Mustang, American Fighter Escort

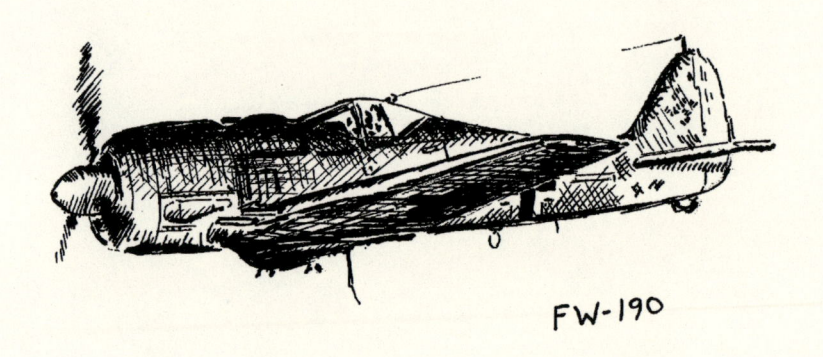

FW-190, Focke-Wulf, German Fighter

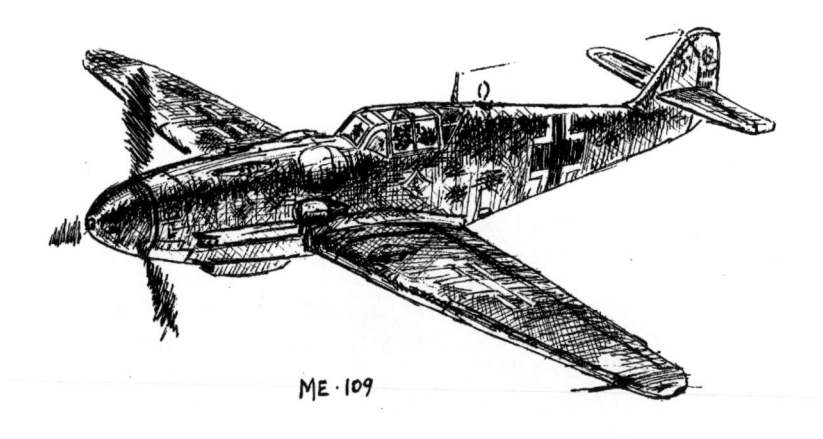

ME-109, Messerschmitt, German Fighter

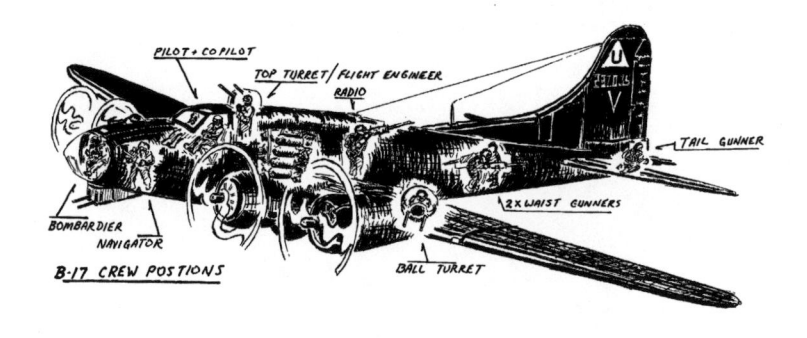

B-17 Crew Positions

Augustine and Esther Fernandez with family celebrating their 50th wedding anniversary, December, 2000.